Smithereens:

Aquitaine, Scotland and Other Meanderings.

Smithereens:

Aquitaine, Scotland
and Other Meanderings.

A Memoir

Basia Gordon

Matador
Unit E2 Airfield Business Park,
Harrison Road, Market Harborough,
Leicestershire. LE16 7UL
Tel: 0116 2792299
Email: books@troubador.co.uk
Web: www.troubador.co.uk/matador
Twitter: @matadorbooks

ISBN 978 1803136 967

British Library Cataloguing in Publication Data.
A catalogue record for this book is available from the British Library.

Printed and bound by CPI Group (UK) Ltd, Croydon, CR0 4YY
Typeset in 11pt Minion Pro by Troubador Publishing Ltd, Leicester, UK

Matador is an imprint of Troubador Publishing Ltd

For Irena and Ziggy
My precioussss ones

Vienne la nuit sonne l'heure
Les jours s'en vont je demeure

(The night falls and the hours ring
The days go away, I remain)

Refrain from "Le Pont Mirabeau", Alcools collection, Guillaume
Apollinaire

Bad days happen to everyone, but when one happens to you, just
keep doing your best and never let a bad day make you feel bad
about yourself.

Big Bird (*Sesame Street*)

Some reviews of Basia Gordon's first memoir

From the River to the Sea: Aquitaine, A Place for Me.
Published 2021.

The memoir is, it seems, the genre of the day. Is it that we are all craving connection with the real lives of others in all intimacy and honesty? Here's a lively, entertaining, vividly detailed, deeply personal account of the ups and downs of a dare-to-dream, labour-of-love, now-or-never, strictly on-a-shoe-string year of a couple renovating a farmhouse in La France Profonde. The Glasgow-born daughter of two Polish exiles, Basia recounts a poignantly European family history whilst weaving the past with the present. I loved the verve and spirit of the book.

Liz Lochhead, poet, playwright, translator, broadcaster, former
Makar, or National Poet of Scotland

Funny and beguiling – sets you right down in rural Aquitaine. You may not want to leave.

Uplifting. The writing effortlessly engaging and evocative but never sentimental.

From The River to the Sea: Aquitaine, A Place for Me... *is a funny, moving memoir about childhood, family and a disappearing way of life.*

A true memoir of life being well lived – with ups and downs, politics, humour & tragedy but always on with a light-hearted note.

From the River to the Sea *is a most enchanting, time-travelling journey, enriched with childhood memories, cultural & culinary adventures, relating the story of a beloved family home, 'Coutal' for over nearly fifty years.*

Aquitaine mon amour – a lockdown memoir inspired by Lot-et-Garonne. A must-read.

If you loved Fidelma Cook's columns from France in this magazine, you will be interested in this tale of a Scottish couple renovating a crumbling farmhouse in the far south-west of the country. Rather like Fidelma's *columns, it offers a blast of sun-soaked escapism while at the same time tackling everything from building disasters to Brexit, wine, food and mud. It's a lively, life-affirming read. Nicely written, too. "There are some choice place names here. Just down the road is the hamlet of Piis. When we drive past the village of Tourette, it is understood everyone has to shout 'F***. It's Tourette!'."*

Garry Scott, *The Herald*, Scotland

CONTENTS

One

Aquitaine Summer 2020 *Glittering*

Is it just happenstance? I am a pragmatic person. There is no expectation of help from any source. No cosmic ordering service for me, no universe coming to my aid. I accept I cannot make all my dreams come true, no matter how hard I may try. But, to come across this signpost, just down the road, innocuously wedged in a concrete slab outside a Glasgow tenement building, seems to be a heaven-sent miracle! How on earth did it land here? Of all the gin joints in all the towns, here is a sign for me, pointing to Coutal Haut, our house buried deep in *La France profonde.* I do a double take. Bergerac and Périgueux on one side and on the other, Bouniagues and Villeneuve-sur-Lot. Hope is floating in the air.

***

Christmas 2019 and Gerry, my partner, and I, are in Coutal Haut once again, much to the disappointment of my daughter, Irena, who has lived in London for the past ten years. 'Mum, when are you going to have Christmas with me?'

'Next year,' I promise. 'We have to go over to Coutal and make sure that all the cedar panelling is properly installed outside the last barn before the weather turns.'

We had spent all of the previous year on sabbatical, working solidly to renovate this "half-island house", a house far from the madding crowd, the house my father had bought nearly fifty years before in Aquitaine. The first thing we had to do was shovel shit from the two barns to create a base for a concrete floor. Although we had tried to do most of the work ourselves to save labour costs, our meagre budget soon ran out and, after a year, we had no option but to return to Glasgow to resume our teaching jobs and replenish the coffers.

On the way down south, driving from Glasgow, Simon, our neighbour and friend in France, had phoned to say that one of our pipes had burst and to phone Saur, the French water agency. He sent a video clip of water gushing out and flooding the place.

By the time we had arrived at our house, Saur had fixed the problem. Simon had brushed the mouse droppings off our bed and switched on the electric blanket. Gerry and I had two days to clean and warm the house and indulge in *les guerres des chariots*, as we refer to the trolley wars in the local supermarket. We successfully wrestled the last bag of Brussel sprouts from a battle-hardened harridan. I carefully unpacked the two huge boxes marked "Christmas" in the garage, cursing us both for our optimism. We had invited our friends Ian, Linda, Jill and Simon, who live nearby, to the full-blown British Christmas in France. As usual, we had underestimated the enormity of the task. I had made a Christmas cake which had tipped over in the car and, on the way, I frantically tried to bash it into shape. In the end, it looked like a thoroughly bashed Christmas cake. There was so much whisky sloshing about in the ingredients that it really didn't matter. My mother had kindly donated Polish Christmas delicacies to make me feel at home. By the time our friends arrived, clutching their most treasured wines, the meal was cooked, the wrapped presents under the tree, and all was right with the world. It was midday and I asked Ian if he would like a drink. He raised one eyebrow. 'Is the sun remotely near the yardarm?' he asked, congenially. I assured him it was.

Two weeks later, all the tasks we had set out to do were done; the weather had been a clement twenty-two degrees, perfect for working outside. We felt smugly satisfied, congratulating ourselves prematurely on the progress we had achieved. 'The year of 2020 will be one of perfect vision,' I said to Gerry.

In the event, we didn't get back to Coutal at Easter 2020 as planned. Who could go anywhere? Partial hibernation is one way to describe Covid Lockdown One, from March to the end of June. We were like tortoises or hedgehogs. It was also a slow process to get to grips with online teaching, but we gradually adjusted to the slower heartbeat of our lives. We felt sure that the summer opening brought the end of the pandemic. Notwithstanding, the measures in France were particularly draconian; if you left your home you had to be armed with an *attestation*, a piece of paper that stipulated you were out only on essential business for one hour maximum. This seemed to satisfy the need for bureaucracy, and those who disobeyed were fined on the spot.

Déjà vu, vu, vu. As soon as a crack appears in the lockdown scenario at the end of June 2020, we tip a few essentials and Rocco the dog into the car and, blinkers on, head south, through Scotland and England, across the Chunnel, Gerry and me alternating the driving. No pootling. Something has triggered a dog memory in Rocco, as he settles down with equanimity in the car. It is as if he is aware that his freedom to roam the range is at the end of his rainbow. *Ouaf ouaf.*

Throughout the lockdown, Linda and Jill, our neighbours in France, were preparing a groovy, psychedelic birthday party for 4 July in Lot-et-Garonne, and I was going to be the third party to the fête. It had nothing to do with American Independence Day; rather it was to be a joint celebration of the three of us turning sixty this year: our own state of independence. I was the hostess with the least to do. Linda was in her element: synchronising accommodation, catering and entertainment. 'Linda loves her spreadsheets,' remarked Jill. One by one, their preparations fell by the wayside, caterers, bands and guests. It was not to be. The tourist flood had turned to a trickle. Our neighbour Anthea said that the upside to having no visitors is that you can swim in your pool naked, with no one to annoy you.

Only one hard-line group refused to capitulate to the unfolding events. Sharon and her sisters, Eunice and Naomi, were on the first early morning flight from Edinburgh to Bordeaux on 4 July 2020. The coming of "The Three Masketeers", armed with all sorts of Covid-preventative equipment. We had been requested to send frequent photographic bulletins of our work before their arrival. *Loving your work!* came back Sharon's approval.

Gerry and I have a week to ensure that the house is aired and cleaned. Or rather the house is *javelisé* – a corruption of the word for a famous cleaning product, *Eau de Javel*. The name sounds much more glamorous than bleach! We hang all the smelly wellingtons upturned on a tree outside and send bulletins about the rubber plantation we are cultivating.

There is nothing like a deadline to get the adrenalin pumping. It doesn't take long to revert to our previous roles as manual workers *extraordinaires*. Gerry concentrates on tiling the second bathroom and finishing the ceiling panel for one bedroom. We can't afford the Travertine tiles for the barn floor that we covet. So instead, I paint the vast expanse bunker green – twice – constantly moving furniture around. With no insulation, the *stoor* floats through the rooftiles in the barn. It needs to be cleaned up constantly. Rocco has his nose pressed to the glass outside, as we toil indoors in the sweltering heat. Occasionally we take him for a constitutional around Lake Tourliac for the full Labrador gambolling. Whilst we work, Rocco amuses himself outside, chasing wildlife or stretching himself out in the sun. A dog's life.

Despite the size of the house, we still have few defined bedrooms, and Gerry and I sleep on the pull-out leather sofa in the barn. To give ourselves the full labourer look, Gerry drops the boot of the car onto my forehead (accidentally). A massive bump impressively dominates the top of my face and we both acquire bleeding and calloused hands.

In the previous autumn, two burnt-out cars had miraculously appeared on the side of the track. When we made enquiries, we discovered that one of the farmers had left them there to encourage the commune to do something about hauling them away. The cars had been left by the people who had rented the ramshackle house next to him throughout the years. Over the last twenty years, constant entreaties to the mayor to remove the cars had fallen on deaf ears, so this was a measure to provoke a response. So far, it was deadlock.

We entered into neighbourly negotiations. We explained first that it was an eyesore. This is not a good approach to persuade people living in the countryside. In the district there is still the reverberation of an almighty *stooshie* thirty years ago when a retired couple from Northern France bought a piece of what they thought was paradise, to live out their remaining years, only to find a pig farm had set up across the road from them. A NIMBY (not in my backyard) offensive ensued, which resulted in the pig farm being shut down. Locals are understandably suspicious of outsiders moving in and upsetting their way of life. We then moved hastily on to the environmental impact of the cars, rusting away on his land. No dice. The countryside is littered with old rust heaps that are eventually reclaimed by nature. Indeed, one of Gerry's hobbies is tramping around and taking photographs of them, especially in the period he was *hors de service* due to his bad back. He called it therapy. Bribery was our last resort. Over the winter, we plied our neighbour with whisky and *tablet*. This had partial success, in that the neighbour moved the cars further up the track, nearer to our home. Cleverly blocking the minor route to Santiago de Compostela. We occasionally witness pilgrims making slow progress to their next stage of pilgrimage, seeking out dwellings with a conch shell carved above the door, signifying welcome and succour. Coutal is resolutely conch shell-free. The car blockage seemed to do the trick. Irate pilgrims complained to the *Mairie*. Anything that may be a barrier to the flocking of tourists was to be avoided. Lo, it came to pass, that one day the offending cars were spirited away. The Lord moves (cars) in mysterious ways.

'God, have you been in a domestic?' enquires Sharon, looking at my lumpen head and bruised limbs. It is time to down tools for a week to enjoy the company of friends. This is what Coutal should be all about, communing with our inner bon viveur. Naomi enjoys herself so much that she extends her stay. This is her first visit here and, as she is a notorious homebody, we are all surprised and delighted. At this point, we are all aware how ill Sharon is. She was diagnosed with lung cancer the previous year. We decide to make the minimum of plans, for she is never sure how she is going to feel at any given time. Indeed, the first evening, she is too unwell to join us in our rolling birthday celebrations. This is a restaurant meal with the usual suspects: Jill, Simon, Linda and Ian. We have been so starved of these moments of conviviality, dining out with friends in beautiful surroundings is to be relished.

As soon as she hears about the *vide grenier*, an upmarket car boot sale, in Monpazier the next day, Sharon whips herself into action. 'Come on, *allez, allez*,' she shouts to her sisters, 'you can't miss this! Bargains to be had!' Monpazier is where we had bought our massive Tabac sign, that was still waiting to be wired up and displayed in central position in the barn. After our long incarceration in Scotland, where *nary a body* stepped out of their doors, the sight of throngs of people in the bright sunlight, with no masks on, jostling in the medieval square, supping in cafés, feels surreal. Eunice, the wise one, mutters, 'This can't be right; there's going to be a backlash at some point.' Ever the optimist, I tell her that there have been zero Covid cases in Vietnam and that France had been strict at the start of the pandemic and was now reaping the benefits.

We stock up on BIBs (bag in a box) of Amblard wine and delicious local produce from the markets and swoon throughout the languorous days with occasional outings. *Tout en modération*, I remind my friends, glugging back another glass of wine. All of us adore cooking; we love to *mitonner*, to cook lovingly.

'Just getting some more from the tittie,' says Sharon, squeezing the last of the Amblard from the box, much to the disapproval of Eunice, who doesn't like such language. We are a bit too coarse for her liking. We love expletives, blasphemy, anthropomorphisms. 'Hey, Eunice, I've got the horn for aubergine fritters!' shouts Sharon. Eunice purses her lips disapprovingly.

Scouring through the attic, we rediscover the 1970's papasan bamboo chairs and resurrect them in the garden: perfect for complete lounging in the sunshine. A photo from 1982 shows a young Sharon lying in one of the chairs listening intently to my grandfather. He is ensconced in another, with a cigarette, as always, clamped to the lower lip, recounting his Siberian tales. 'No! Not the Gulag again!' I would say, laughingly, my hands clamped over my ears. We uncover a pack of photos of all the children on the bamboo, striking various poses.

Gerry discovers two *claies* – the old plum dryers – and pops them under his feet, perfect snowshoes. He spends a happy morning perfecting his moves.

Robert and Nicola (London friends who have a house nearby) have appeared, and we join their bubble. Nicola shows me how to dive, by diving perfectly through a rubber ring in the swimming pool. 'But what if I get stuck?' I ask anxiously.

'You won't get stuck,' she reassures me. 'Give it a shot.' I try to conjure up the picture of a doughnut, luring me in, but it's no good. I bellyflop ignominiously and stick to the breaststroke.

Sitting outside in a restaurant we are suddenly waylaid by an Englishman wearing a tweed woollen facemask with sweat dripping down his jowls. 'You come over here from England, spreading your germs and don't wear masks!' he harangues. Not quite accurate: we have all been here for at least some weeks in isolation. We have property in the area. We are outside and most of us are not English. However, he is right, in some respects; we have been lulled, by our own volition, into a false sense of security. I think the haranguer would have gone ballistic if he knew that the boys had been swimming naked in the medieval well under Jennie and Ron's home in Castillonnès.

We are aware that our halcyon days are numbered, that the spell will soon be broken, that the future is not orange. One evening we decide to don our kaftans, turn the music up and waft around the barn. 'You know I don't like to gossip…but… draw your chairs closer…' cackles Sharon conspiratorially. 'God, you leech indiscretion,' sighs Naomi.

Eunice adds, 'Loose lips sink ships.' Apparently, according to Eunice, our sino-oracle, the Chinese character denoting the act of quarrelling depicts two women; if it depicts three women, it means the act of gossiping. There are four of us – me, Sharon, Eunice and Naomi – and the night is young.

We are well oiled by the never-ending flow of nectar from the BIBs when I bite into a brazil nut and, almost immediately, my lips swell to Mick Jagger liver lips consistency and my throat tightens. I struggle to breathe. 'I'll be alright,' I rasp, like a nineteenth-century maiden, 'just bring me over the smelling salts.' My attendants are having none of this; next I will be calling out for laudanum. I am bundled into the car, my head on Eunice's lap as she strokes my face and whispers reassuringly, whilst Gerry has sobered up completely and hurtles the car across the narrow country roads to the hospital in Villeneuve. We float into the *Urgences*, the Accident and Emergency unit, still in our colourful kaftans, like some demented exotic birds, much to the astonishment of those in the waiting room. The receptionist takes one look at me and in *deux minutes* I am in a room with a nurse and a doctor, whirling around me. The sheer bliss of the oxygen mask. I shut my eyes.

'I see you have come for your yearly check-up,' says the doctor, sternly, looking at his notes. It is more than a year since I was admitted into the same hospital in the same state of distress. He checks how far I live from Villeneuve. I promise that I will have a complete check-up when I go back to Glasgow. I promise that I will never be more than half an hour from a hospital until such time. I will make sure that I always have an EpiPen on my person in the event of another anaphylactic episode. I would have promised to eat a kilo of unpeeled lemons every day, to be released. I must learn to take care of myself and not to take risks. When friends tell me that I should not worry, it is perfectly safe for me to come into their houses because they have cleaned every room thoroughly and there is not a speck of cat dander around, I have to be clear and say no, I can't. I must be firm. I have never experienced a peaceful stay in a cat-inhabited house.

Sharon is fast asleep, and Naomi is still up, hugging the dog, when we return, exhausted, in the early hours of the morning. All evidence of merriment has vanished.

I hadn't known about Naomi's "Marie Kondo" tendencies. The following day, when Sharon and I are *hors de combat*, she whisks around the kitchen like a dervish. For many years, the kitchen has been in dire need of a clean-out. The sink has been made for dwarves which results in a sore back if you are there for any length of time. Naomi cannot believe the amount of replication of items, and I am not allowed to see or rifle through the plastic bags of objects outside the door. At last, I am guided into the kitchen with a blindfold for the "big reveal". I weep with gratitude and amazement; it looks tidy, clean and uncluttered! The elves have been here! Pleased with the response, Naomi spends the next few days in a flurry of chucking out and scouring surfaces. She teaches me how to fold and store laundry. She has an untapped talent for storage solutions. I realise that I still need domestic training. Or maybe I just need a cleaner to help me, I reason to myself.

'Well, it was about time,' I squeak hoarsely to Sharon. I am in bed in the living room and she is in one of the barn bedrooms. There is a gap in the stone wall so we can shout at each other and be heard.

I shout: 'It was all attention-seeking on your part. You're not the only ill person in the village! You're just lazy!'

Sharon shouts back: 'I told you being ill is hard work!' Sharon can shout at me with greater ease, rather than the other way round. My throat feels like a badger's bum.

'And, by the way,' my squeak turns into a gravelly growl, '*j'accuse!* See you and your co-conspirator, Katy,' our pet name for my daughter Irena, 'I intercepted the letter – with *photos* – you two sent to *What Not to Wear*.' This was a popular TV programme twenty-odd years ago, whereby some poor creature was nominated by her nearest and dearest and knocked into sartorial shape by the two bossy presenters, one of whom lived next door to Sharon in Battersea at the time.

'Just trying to help a soul in need,' retorts Sharon, airily.

I warm to my theme. 'You're such a *cheeky bizom*! Katy wrote that the reason she was nominating me was that I had no dress sense whatsoever and I was an embarrassment!'

Sharon answers, 'Well, no word of a lie there...'

By this time, I am shouting, 'This is what you wrote, you *traitor.*' I read from a bit of paper I have extracted from the bottom of my bag: 'This would be your most challenging subject yet. Trust me. Her worst outfit: red fleece and blue maternity pants (whilst not pregnant) and K Skips shoes circa 1985.'

Sharon is having none of it. 'You are so ungrateful. You can't go out looking like a dog's dinner.'

I answer, apropos of nothing, 'For your information, in dog years, you are dead!' I adopt a mournful look and add: 'She died in his arms... but only after a struggle.'

Sharon laughs. '*Yer nae yuis tae naebdae if yer deid.*' In other words, you are no use to anyone if you are dead. 'Just to let you know, there is *tons* of life in the old dog yet. Just saying.' And with that, we both splutter. Nurse Eunice runs between her two demanding patients, dispensing medication, ministrations, porridge and ice cream, plumping up pillows, taking orders. Meanwhile, Skivvy Naomi is hell-bent on her house-cleaning mission. Naomi rarely sits down; her eagle eye is always on the prowl for some rearranging/sorting/cleaning. This house must be paradise for her. Gerry, meanwhile, is outside building a wood store for firewood. Rocco is in his fur coat and lying splat on the terrace. The heat is too much for him. He has stabbed his right eye on a stick and looks sorry for himself. Gerry comes out of the garage with news of more visitors. Apparently, a snake has made its home in the top of the chest of drawers in the far corner. He is getting nice and fat. 'It's like a penthouse suite,' says Gerry. 'Why would he move? There is a never-ending supply of mice living in the lower drawers and they are too stupid to clear out.' It's true, the lucky snake has a living larder that is constantly replenished. Now, whenever we have to go into the garage, we make sure we make as much noise as possible, banging on the metal doors with a baseball bat, to let the visitors know that humans are coming in for a brief moment, just to fetch something, but don't worry, normal life will resume soon.

An argument erupts between Eunice and Gerry, one evening. It is to do with politics, but no one now remembers the *actualité*. What is recalled, is that neither side backs down and eventually, Naomi, Sharon and I retreat indoors to let them slug it out like hares boxing each other. They are equally stubborn, but happily, both pronounce triumphantly hours later, 'I won!'

Once The Three Masketeers have flown back to the land of pestilence, Gerry and I return to our labours, moving medieval beams into the back bedroom, sealing floors and erecting the scaffolding, so Gerry can work on his "Sistine Chapel" as he calls it. This is the massive task he has set himself to insulate the barn ceiling. I go back to my bucolic ways, picking and drying lavender and rosemary, filtering the walnut wine, twice, and turning myself a pleasing shade of nut brown in the warm sun.

We catch up with our neighbours, Étienne and Suzanne, now in their nineties, who complain that their cleaner has decided to retire. She is a spring chicken who is only seventy-one years old. They are both happy though. Their ruse of tricking the hedgehogs, hell-bent on stealing the eggs from the hencoop, has succeeded. They have done this by placing plastic eggs and lightbulbs instead of real eggs in their place. Meanwhile, every time we meet Ron, our neighbour down the road, he invariably asks us if we would like to partake of a pickled egg.

Étienne asks what Rocco does. I am rather perplexed. 'He's a dog,' I reply. 'He just hangs around.'

Étienne persists. 'Can he go hunting, looking for truffles, at least guard the house?' No, I have to admit, he doesn't do any of these things; he is a pet. Étienne shakes his head. He doesn't understand the concept.

The *repas nocturnes*, the communal evening meals in the village, have now resumed. Nonetheless, apart from one evening in Monflanquin, we tend to just stick with our "bubble" people and continue the merriment in our own backyard.

We take Rocco to get his vaccination for the return trip and the vet remarks that he still has his Scottish coat on despite the heat! There is hardly any room for him in the car once we pile in the BIBs and garlic plaits and he curls himself around the massive glass fruit bowl Sharon insisted on buying in the *vide grenier* in Monpazier. In Calais, Rocco eyes up the ferret in front of him in the pet passport queue. He is looking fetching. Up to this point, I had not known that cats, dogs, rabbits and ferrets were the only pets allowed through water borders. The ferret is not bothered and gives Rocco a look as if to say, *Don't even think about it, son. My human will batter you if you do.*

Back to Glasgow and the bubble bursts.

If only I could bottle these precious days and pop them on the shelf beside the walnut wine. 2020. The summer before everything fell apart.

Two

Churchill & Gladstone *Dusk*

New Year 2021. My life is in a state of disarray. I am growing old. Nora Ephron was right when she said that at this age, and I paraphrase, we are only one step from being a bag-lady. Perhaps it's just as well we do not know what the future holds for us all.

Life here in Scotland is meandering on at a snail's pace: a very old, sluggish snail weighed down by the shell of its home. It's lockdown and no-one is going anywhere. I'm travelling in my mind, a terrific distance, walking up the muddy track to Coutal Haut, dragging somnolence in my wake, checking the postbox on the way home. Five *punaises*, a desiccated fly and a few damp letters and bills. It is winter and very still, almost sterile. No lingering smell of mint and lavender in the air; no pungent stink of duck guano. Leafdrifts pile up outside the door. Rose branches detached from their moorings hang limply on the walls. Wisteria tries forcefully to latch itself onto limestone.

Just as well that you put down the stones on the driveway, wrote Linda, our neighbour, *it has been so muddy, it has been tricky to get to the house. Stout wellies required.*

I'm not going in.

I have not been here since the summer before, and the year of pestilence drags on. There is no point in disturbing the gaiety inside; the mice are having their indoor field day, lounging around, a study of insouciance, scratching their tummies, knitting balaclavas, generously distributing their droppings in a nonchalant manner, snacking on *foosty* leather shoes and books and magazines (they can fairly skim through) and snoozing fitfully. Somehow, they have found a source of sustenance, a forgotten bag of dog food, and life is good. The stone martens, *les fouines*, are gyrating sinuously round the central beam in the barn, as the dormice, *les loirs*, look down on the mayhem from their eyrie high up in the wall, their huge eyes wide with wonderment.

Delicately embroidered cobwebs like antimacassars festoon every nook and cranny, linking the oak beams and Christmas glass baubles still hanging down from the windows after two years. Difficult to see through the windows; I never did get round to cleaning them, deeming the job low priority.

I note that the *loirs* have not yet managed to topple the gargoyles we had jammed in the ledges of the stone walls.

My head is full of images of Sharon: her long, thin face and mischievous green eyes.

The track to Coutal Haut is now my own Via Dolorosa. No longer with the life force that was Sharon. She would have countered impatiently, 'Get off that cross; I need the wood.'

Nothing will ever be the same again. Everything about her is now retrospective. When we were young and dreaming about the future, we knew what the beginning was; we had an inkling what the middle would bring, how it would all unfold, but we didn't know the precise date of the end. There are only two days in your life that are less than twenty-four hours long. Maybe there is an infinitesimal possibility that this might not be the case. We only know about a whole person's life once it is over. There are two metaphors I can recall capturing the moment of death: a helicopter flying into a mountainside and a light switch turned off.

Suddenly, the splendour and clamour of life is muted. Oh, there are bursts of brilliance that shine through. Our last Burns Supper in Coutal Haut with my daughter Irena, her fiancé Ant and our friend Noaimh, who had flown over from London. Sharon stood tall, bedecked in tartan, Gucci belt cinched at her waist, and sang, clear as a bell:

'Ae fond kiss
Fare-thee-well, thou first and fairest!
Fair-thee-well, thou best and dearest!
Thine be ilka joy and treasure
Peace Enjoyment Love and Pleasure!'

Sharon standing against the Apartheid Wall in Bethlehem, flicking through a copy of *Vogue*, "Shazza" graffitied behind her, defiant to the last. Nonchalance personified.

Sharon running up the road, arms outstretched. '*Darlink!*'

Sharon was fastidious in so many ways. 'You know, Fran,' she said to our friend, 'when you wear earrings, make sure your hair is cut back so you can see your ears.' Hours would be spent choosing the *right* accessories for the *right* outfit. Her standards were always exacting; her language always precise: fruity and frequently peppered with expletives. Work would burn through her hands. Every day was packed to the gunnels with things to accomplish. 'I love to wake early to welcome the day,' she often said.

Apart from a lifelong addiction to Tunnock's teacakes and pineapple cakes, a sweet tooth legacy of her Scottish heritage, she was an adventurous cook. Nothing gave her more pleasure than to entertain friends with long and boozy epicurean Mediterranean spreads bursting with colour, texture and flavour.

She craved to be an interior decorator but needed to continue in high-powered, financially rewarding jobs to provide the lifestyle to which she aspired. Her son, Will, complained, 'I've spent half my life living under dustsheets in houses being pulled apart.'

She fired back: 'Do you think I love troubleshooting, working with all those macho types, with their polyurethane-soled shoes, always looking behind my back for some young buck to replace me? I have to do what I do to earn the dosh; there's no old Aunt Matilda going to leave me a thatched cottage any time soon.' And it was true. She was the complete self-made woman, coming from a council flat in Greenock and clawing her way up the corporate world.

Sharon's London townhouse was testimony to her keen eye and discerning taste. "Adding value", she would justify every embellishment. We were forever foraging in art galleries and shows. 'I have just got Chairman Mao framed in special non-reflective glass. He is just the dog's bollocks.'

'*Morgen!* What are you up to?' I'd phone up and ask.

'Oh, you know, just perving some interior decoration magazines. I've got the horn for these divine designer door handles... they are just amazeballs!' Sharon's conversation would be shot through with her distinct turns of phrase and her favourite adjectives of the season, some pinched from her children. 'Yuk, that's sooo moist.' After so many years in London, her clear voice had taken on a London cadence. 'Ow, I kneoow...'

As Eunice, her sister, said, 'It's Lady Diana had a banana.' Sharon would always revert to the full Scottish burr, to forcibly put her points across in work scenarios. There would be many a pipsqueak shaking in his/her *breeks*.

'Firm, but fair,' she would intone. Every few days, we would download all the saved-up tittle-tattle for a satisfying bitchathon session. Frequently, we would buoy ourselves up for the working day with a pep talk. Me sitting in my parked car outside the school in Glasgow, Sharon invariably travelling to work in London. Our conversation would come in staccato. 'Just going down into the tube, going through a tunnel in a minute.'

'*Courage mon brave*, don't let the buggers grind you down! Do you think we will ever get early parole? Please release me, let me go!'

It was no surprise that she leapt on Coutal Haut as a project in waiting, once the London house had been completely gutted and renovated. The trouble was that her suggestions were way beyond what we could afford. 'Basia, why don't you just get this kitchen island for £35k? A bargain!' One dark October morning, we woke up to a lorry pulling up outside the house and a disgruntled driver falling out of his cabin.

'This is the fourth Coutal I have been to! I was about to give up!' He then disgorged two nineteenth-century dressers, seagrass carpet, candlesticks and various accoutrements.

'This is just the start!' laughed Sharon. 'This is the party house now! This will be the jewel in the crown!' Sharon was generous with her possessions, time and friendship.

Returning to Glasgow after a year of merriment and furious activity was a bit of a damp squib. The house was far from finished and our debts were mounting after our sabbatical year, but luckily, we had teaching jobs to which we could return.

Before leaving Coutal Haut, at the end of the summer, Sharon complained of a sore side. When she returned to London, she was given the jaw-dropping diagnosis: stage four liver and lung cancer. 'What the *fuck* just happened?' said Sharon. 'I'm a vegetarian that has looked after body and soul! I *demand* a steward's inquiry into this. I *don't* accept this!' I countered that it was just greed on her part; just one cancer was not enough. 'This is going to be a tough paper round,' she conceded. 'But I am determined to live; so much to do, so little time.' She corrected herself: 'So much to do, so few people to do it for me.'

She concentrated all her efforts on renovating her recently acquired house in Edinburgh. (There was always one challenge too many.) 'I'm not leaving the party until it is absolutely perfecto and fabulous,' she said, firmly. Several years previously, for her fiftieth birthday, we had organised a big party in a Spanish-themed venue in the middle of Glasgow. The night before, she complained of a slight pain in her side.

'Och, you're fine; stop your nonsense,' proclaimed her no-nonsense sister, Eunice. 'You probably had too many Quavers. You are dehydrated. Glug down some water.'

The morning after, following the usual falling-out with her daughter, Sharon whispered, 'Honestly, I'm not feeling too good.' Eunice whipped her off to the hospital, where she was immediately diagnosed with a burst appendix. 'I told you I wasn't feeling great,' she accused us, vindicated, from her hospital bed.

There is something that nags me about this memory. Sharon recounted a funny story about one of the women, lying in the bed opposite her. She sounded like a pugnacious bruiser, but I can't remember the story itself. I could contact her sisters and ask them if they can remember the tale, but that is the point – I want to ask Sharon personally and I now have only my fading faculties to rely on. I realise dumbly, this will be forever until I too die.

This is why I write about her. This is a person I want everyone to remember. There is almost a year between us, give or take a few days. December babies, born in the wake of Christmas. I will always be the older one. This year will now expand to two years, three years; the absence will widen, who knows for how long?

Even Sharon's resilience and sheer determination could not stop the carnage ripping through her body. Photos of flooded lungs, protuberances sticking out of her head and other parts, skin grafts; all were sent over fast and furious. *Waterboarded again! Eek, something else has just popped out! Clock the triffid (pillar cyst) growing out of my bonce! It looks like I've got an antenna!*

Or a teletubby has taken up residence? I ventured.

I've got my moon face back from too many steroids, she moaned. *I'm girding my loins for the next round... you know what's coming next... I'd better get my pampers on...* Death greedily crept into her body like a thief in the night, stealing her organs, whilst the vultures patiently flew overhead.

We were both equally amazed and flabbergasted by the body's seeming ability to mutate into an alien being.

Her family were called into hospital to say goodbye when she caught Covid. 'No thanks, no goodbyes; this is not going to happen,' she dismissed the bewildered staff, looking like aliens themselves in their Hamzat suits. 'I don't care if you think I should be grateful because these are exceptional circumstances.' She sniffed.

'People keep on coming in and out my room, telling me terrible things. Oh God, I've got Nurse Ratched on my tail again!'

'OK, calm down. What's she done this time?' I asked.

Sharon was indignant. 'She said that I should get my affairs in order. There's no hope. I think she's saying I'm toast. She said that the cancer has spread and now I have a telescoped bowel and if they operate, I will probably die, *but* if, by some miracle, I survive, then I will have two colostomy bags. *And* even worse,' she added darkly, 'she pronounced my name *Shaaaaron* not *Shayron*.' We all knew that this was a faux pas in extremis.

The Lancet, the venerable medical journal, asked if they could publish a paper about Sharon, as a liver and lung cancer patient who survived Covid. This gave her untold satisfaction. 'See,' she crowed, 'I have confounded medical expectations! See you, Nurse Ratched!'

'Yes,' I agreed and solemnly declared, 'you are Lady Lazarus.'

The hospice where she spent her last few months met with her approval. 'Could I move in?' I asked. 'It's like a first-class hotel. I'll just pop in a camp bed by the window; no one will notice...'

'Yes, it's divine, sooooo peaceful; although I would tweak the colour scheme – it's a tad bland,' answered Sharon. I was not surprised to discover that many of the staff were volunteers. All people, who I realise now, had also gone through the grief of the death of a loved one and hence wanted to ease the pain of the others going through a similar experience.

'Are you a relative?' asked one of the nurses, looking at me with disapproval.

'Yes, she is. She's my cousin. *So leave us alone!*' Sharon was not to be trifled with.

'Umm, the minister is here – would you like to speak to her, about, umm, arrangements?'

'No, I certainly would not. I am far too busy. I've still to finish the upstairs in my house.' Sharon was adamant.

'The minister is from Greenock, so I thought…' The nurse's voice tailed off as she met the full force of Sharon's glare.

'That'll be a double *no* then!' The nurse scurried out.

'What do you think about the stairs?' Sharon turned to me, showing photos of her bespoke oak treads. 'Only £11k, well worth it. Took ages to pull all that together. And I have sourced the perfect tiles…'

The nurses and staff all adored funny and exuberant Sharon. 'Is there anything you would like?' they asked anxiously.

Sharon nodded. 'Well, funny you should ask, yes, there is. I'd like you to arrange art lessons for me.'

'Art lessons?' The nurses looked puzzled. 'No one has ever asked for them before.'

'They have now,' answered Sharon firmly.

Two weeks before she died, she married her long-term boyfriend, Rob. Only once they had exchanged their vows were they allowed to remove their facemasks and kiss each other. She looked beautiful, as she walked into the registry office with the piper playing "Amazing Grace". Dougal, her beloved hairpiece, gave her hair a luxuriant, shiny bounce. ('Why,' she asked, 'was I not given the Dolly Parton advice on the power of wigs when I was younger?') Once back at the hospice, the staff crowded around and asked to see her ring. She proudly twirled it around her finger.

'So, what are the other inmates in the exit house like?' I asked.

'Well,' she answered, 'I've never met any of the other patients,' she tittered. 'They are as quiet as the grave! But the nurses give me all the gossip about them. For example, her next door was saying how nice the food is. And then she asked what the Christmas lunch is like!' By this time, we were both wheezing with laughter.

'No, she didn't!'

'Yes!' Sharon nodded gleefully. 'Can you imagine?'

'Do you remember when you had to travel all the way on the train from London to Glasgow, with your clothes and your gold shoes spattered in blood?' she asked.

Sharon had hosted a wild Hallowe'en party and we had got up the next morning the worse for wear. Sharon had a big swollen lump in the middle of her forehead, rather like a Cyclops, after walking straight into the massive glass doors of her new extension. ('Far too clean,' I argued, 'what did you expect?') We covered the glass with hazard tape, so it did look as if we were preparing for a crime scene. Gerry and I had invited friends over for breakfast, so just as we had cleared the detritus from the night before, the doorbell rang, and there stood our friends, Dana and Tiago. At that precise moment, a huge scream pierced the air. Patricia, the Spanish au pair, had tripped down the stairs in her pyjamas. Dana and Tiago (the would-be guests) were smartly dismissed (breakfast cancelled); Patricia had concussion and blood started to drip down the side of her head. We bundled her up in my dressing gown and Sharon drove me, Patricia and Gerry to the A&E with Patricia resting her bleeding head on my lap, before rushing back to look after Will, her son. Eventually, Patricia was stitched up, but time was flying by, and we had to catch the train back to Glasgow so that we would be back in time for work the next day. Luckily, I had our train tickets in my handbag, and we managed to get onto the train at Kings Cross, just as it was leaving. It was immediately as we sat down that we became aware of the shocked faces of the passengers. We looked like the doppelgangers of Nancy Spungen and Sid Vicious of the Sex Pistols. Inadvertently, I had tried to wipe off some blood with my hand and left a big streak on my cheek. How does one explain to the curious onlookers? Best not to even try!

Sharon clapped her hands with glee. 'That's the spirit! More misadventures!'

Sharon had brought her favourite unguents with her to the hospice, but she never failed to give us a list of further requirements. 'I wouldn't mind some rhubarb custards,' a type of confectionary from childhood days, 'and whilst you are in town, could you track down some Caudalie body oil?' Caudalie is a famous spa outside Bordeaux, where they also manufacture a skincare range using the residue of grape skins. We were addicted to their products. I duly sourced some Caudalie body oil, aptly named "Huile Divine", and gave her a gentle massage. 'Ah, that's fabulous, but could you stop tickling my feet?'

'Your Majesty, I am not tickling your feet.' I breathed in her ear. ''Tis merely the flames licking your sides.'

'*You fucking bitch*! I am going to *kill* you!' Sharon screamed. We were both convulsed with laughter but wrenched with indescribable pain. How could this be the end? How could all these years, all these confidences, these adventures, just disappear? Nearly forty years of love and friendship suddenly extinguished. We could say absolutely anything to each other, and it wouldn't matter. There was no filter. From nose-singing in Kazakhstan to the complete all-over body waxing of today's youth. 'Smooth and hairless, you could run a silk scarf over their bodies. Edward Scissorhands. Pubic topiary,' she opined. 'Not free and wild as in our day...' From levity to gravity, or as Sharon would probably have said, "from levitas to gravitas and back again".

Our last conversations were about the loss of bowel control. I would ask her: 'Anything else fallen off today, ma'am?' There was no end to the tales of the mini disasters as her body disintegrated. I reminded her of my experience of colonic irrigation. At the time, it was the ultimate body cleansing thing to do. 'Honestly, Sharon, once they had shoved the pipe up my *bahookie* and got the water flowing, I knew it was a bad idea; I couldn't get out of the clinic fast enough.' Once on the street, I could feel that an accident was imminent, so I crouched down and relieved myself behind bushes on the side of Great Western Road, to the consternation and amusement of drivers in their cars flashing past. They are not the only ones who can flash. It's just the envelope we live in, isn't it? I reasoned.

'Now this is where I would like Rob to take me to,' said Sharon, excitedly, showing me photos of the Buchanan Arms Hotel up in the Highlands. 'Doesn't it remind you of the Hotel Pulitzer in Amsterdam?' We had spent her fortieth birthday in this chic hotel which also doubled as a mini art gallery. Her face fell. 'But Rob said there's no point in taking me to any more hotels, as I just start snoozing on the sofa from about 5pm.' Rob had been very caring throughout her last year. When she was in perky mode, he would take her to chic hotels and, as she said, be her "McMillan nurse".

On my recommendation, they visited Ashford Castle in Cong, County Mayo in Ireland. Rob is Irish, so he was happy to go anywhere in his beloved homeland. The castle is well known as a luxury venue and the backdrop for the 1952 John Wayne film, *The Quiet Man*. Ten years ago, I attended my cousin Lena's wedding there and forevermore Sharon would beseech me: '*Bashoo!* Tell the story again!' It never failed to titillate.

My cousins – Lena, Sarah and Zeina – were born and brought up in Beirut. They are half-Scottish and half-Lebanese (this is another story) but I know them well, as they stayed in Glasgow off and on when the fighting in the seventeen-year-long civil war became unbearable. We have met up many times around the world since. Indeed, Sharon, our friend Susan and I visited Lena and Zeina in Dublin, as a weekend escape from small, irritating children, and they took us to a Lebanese restaurant one evening. The next day we were taken for a trip around boggy countryside, feeling very sick and hungover. Puce was the order of the day. This didn't stop Sharon cutting business deals on the phone as she barked, 'Just take a million from that budget,' as Susan and I threw up out of the windows.

Lena was marrying an Irish chap, Patrick, who has five sisters. It hadn't been easy to find a priest who would join an Irish Catholic and a Muslim together in holy matrimony, but eventually, the old doddering and tipsy Father Ted was found. It was a small wedding of forty guests in the chapel in the castle grounds. Father Ted was extremely inebriated by the start of the ceremony. 'You are all welcome here; we are all God's children,' he slurred. 'It's lovely to welcome people from all over the world – we have the Irish, the Scottish, the Polish and the Lebanese. All one big happy family.' His voice lowered as he looked accusingly at the Polish contingency. 'Well, it would have been if some *Pole* had not come over and killed our folk in a car accident!' (This was reference to a horrific car accident which had happened the previous day. I hasten to add that the aforementioned *Pole* had nothing to do with the wedding party.) The Polish contingency shuffled uncomfortably in their seats. 'But there you have it.' He brightened up. 'And all the way from Lebanon, my, now, that is exotic, that is. Now tell me, Lena, when you get back to Beirut, will you be stoned for marrying a non-Muslim?' I thought my Uncle Abed was going to have a massive heart attack. My Aunt Janet gripped his hand tightly.

'You missed out the pervasive smell in the castle,' accused Sharon.

'The most wonderful lavender polish,' I answered. Sharon was satisfied.

'Do you remember,' Sharon asked, the *szkocki bicze* – "the Scottish beating"?' Again, this was a reference to our frequent trips to Poland, over twenty-five years, with or without children. After visiting friends and relatives in Warsaw and Krakow, we would invariably find ourselves in Brenna, a holiday resort in the Carpathian Mountains beside the Czech border where my Uncle Wojtek and Aunt Kasia have a beautiful wooden house. My aunt would fuss and coddle us, checking out spa treatments in the sanatorium close by. One such treatment piqued our curiosity: the *szkocki bicze*. Let's not ask what it is, we foolishly decided, let's have a surprise. We shivered in our bikinis and awaited our fate. We were taken one by one, made to stand against a wall, then a hefty man gleefully hosed us down with icy water as we desperately ran up and down trying to escape the full waterfall. This was much, much more than the ice bucket challenge. This was just unadulterated sadism. When we told my uncle all about it later, he laughed.

'I bet you felt alive!' My uncle is a macho man; this treatment would appeal to him.

My uncle is also prone to fits of melancholia. One day, we found him crying outside his beautiful home, which he had built himself, and the immaculate garden with flowers which he and my aunt tended with loving care. 'Why did your father not live to see this?' Despair was in his voice. He had idolised his older brother. My father had died long before the Berlin

Wall had come down and had never visited Communist Poland, Soviet-controlled Poland nor post-Communist Poland. He had not grown old.

My mother did the same thing. A year after my father had died, I found her crying in the orchard at Coutal Haut, bemoaning the fact that my father was not there on this lovely sunlit day, in the house he had dreamed of.

And I too, will think of Sharon, in this house she loved, in the same way.

'Do you remember? Do you remember?' asked Sharon insistently.

I digress. I digress because I am desperate. I am desperate because I want her heart to keep on pumping, her lungs to suck air in and out like bellows, her blood to flow through her veins, her mind untrammelled and unclouded; all synapses working in complete alignment. Is this it now for the survivors, the apogee of anecdotage? If only we could summon up the past and relive it all again. Instead, the days, months and years push us forward inexorably into the unknown.

I don't want to go up this muddy track to Coutal Haut alone. I want Sharon to be here with me. I want the sunflowers to be out, like bright yellow lanterns shining our way home. I want to hear the peal of her laughter again. I want to see the green colour of her eyes.

Sharon texted on 29 September 2020. *Darling, I am going to try and break free today. I want to go home. Xxx.* Feisty to the end, she delivered a two-finger salute to the grim reaper.

All our dreams pulverised, smithereens.

***

A few years earlier, on one of our trips to Shoreditch, we spotted a pottery workshop and the sign on the window advertising death masks. 'Well, that would be a wheeze – let's do it!' we whooped delightedly. It was the best facemask ever, the complete revivification process, as we were each smothered with green clay, straws poking out of our noses.

'My skin is glowing, and so is yours!' said Sharon, approvingly, patting my cheeks. We tried to persuade my daughter Irena to have the same done, but she went down a slightly different route and had a copy of her torso cast, which now sits proudly on her shelves.

'I reasoned it was best to show my breasts when they were still in tip-top condition.' The vanity of youth. Sharon and I looked at each other, crestfallen.

'Too late for that, hen,' she sighed, looking at me. 'We are no spring chickens.' We cheered up when we eventually picked up our masks. They looked just like Gladstone and Churchill: one a thin, long face and one a round, fat face. Laurel and Hardy. It was impossible to know whether we were young or old.

***

October 2020. Driving to Edinburgh for Sharon's funeral, my Pussy Riot brooch pinned on my collar, I suddenly let out a shriek of pain. I had squirted Olbas Oil into my eye instead of eye drops. Immediately, my right eye swelled up into a red, pulsating tomato. 'I can go back now,' said Gerry, anxiously.

'No, no, keep on driving,' I spluttered. 'We mustn't be late.' The mobile pinged a text message: *Blessings on her journey home.* I looked at it unbelievingly, with my blood-soaked eye. Sharon would have been incensed by the sentiment; she had fought so hard to stay alive. That was not the home she wanted to go to; she was running in the opposite direction.

'At least let me see sixty,' she had pleaded. 'Surely, it's not so much to ask. Or at least let me get match fit for Ziggy's wedding.' Ziggy is my footballer son. She was in full flight and full flow to the end, totally lucid. Not for her, the decrepitude and confusion of old age.

Our friend Susan was driving in her car ahead of us. Due to Covid restrictions, there were strictly twenty named people allowed to attend, which meant that, after the family, there were just a few places for friends. Nevertheless, Susan hoped she would be allowed to attend in the event of someone not being able to turn up. If all else failed, she would just wait outside. When Susan visited Sharon a few months before, she remarked, 'She is the one that's ill, but when you leave her, you feel so buoyed up. She always makes you feel good.'

The motorway ground to a halt. A car burst into flames in front of us and another had broken down. Desperately, I tried to flick from one radio station to the other to find out what was happening. There was a thirty-mile tailback; no one was going anywhere.

'We are going to miss Sharon's funeral,' I wailed.

Gerry said quietly, 'You are lucky you are not the person in the crash.'

That sobered me up. He exited the motorway and weaved through the small towns around Edinburgh, parked the car and we ran into St Mary's Cathedral. We had missed most of the service. The cathedral is so huge that twenty people look lost inside it, separated out, with their masks on. We were all participants in some grotesque masked ball. Ready to begin. We could hardly make out our fellow mourners at the far end of the cathedral as we walked in; for one dreadful moment, I thought we had come to the wrong place. 'How come you got a cathedral?' I asked Eunice later.

'Sharon had said she wanted somewhere with smells and bells in it. Anyway, as it happened, most of the churches were closed. So, in desperation, I thought, why not try the cathedral? I could hardly believe it when they said yes. Apparently, no one thinks that the cathedral is available.' Sharon would have approved. So many times, we walked up the road from Haymarket Station past this cathedral to her new flat conversion snuggled in a cobbled street, a throwback to the 1930s, just round the corner from the sign in the grounds of the Museum of Modern Art, "There will be no miracle here". The view from the flat is of a Bentley sign on one of the cottages across the road and the sound is the Water of Leith flowing past. Sharon had spent the last year ripping it apart and turning it into a stylish state of the art modern home, meeting her exacting standards.

In the recent past, Gerry and I have attended this cathedral for two completely different events. The first was a gathering with other Palestinian supporters around the Awda Key, a giant bronze key outside the main entrance symbolising the keys of stolen Palestinian homes. The second event was a concert to commemorate one hundred years of Polish independence. The cathedral was packed; a light show lit up the ceiling; the lush chords of music and singers reverberated around the walls.

What a contrast to this solemn, low-key event. No voices fill the vast expanse; Covid restrictions do not allow singing; and we listen to the organ play the hymns which would have pleased Sharon's recently deceased Pentecostal parents. Sharon's taste of music was eclectic, and I think of all the songs she would have chosen. Recently, I have come across people, alive and dead, who have made their funeral music selection. The ones that come to mind are Louis Armstrong's "What A Wonderful World", Edith Piaf's "Non, je ne regrette rien" and the inspirational "Y Viva España". Sharon left no instructions.

She did not go into the good night gently. For her, it was lust for life. She is gone and we are the ones left behind, finding our comforts where we can. There is a song called *"She's not there"* by The Zombies going around my head like ticker tape.

This is the third Covid funeral I have attended in the last few months. There is no luxury of hugs and comforting words; we are all separated in our own painful bubbles.

We arrive too late to hear the minister's words, or the tribute given by another of Sharon's friends who is a university professor. Apparently, the words "fuck" and "cunt" were mentioned on several occasions, casually tossed into the holy sanctum by the academic, much to the consternation of the minister and Sharon's Aunt Ella. It was completely inappropriate.

We do manage to hear her daughter Amelia say: 'This cathedral would have been full – at the drop of a hat two hundred people would have flown in from all over the world to say goodbye to my mum. Those of my mum's friends who contacted me said so many positive things about her, but the words that come to mind are that she was her own woman, a strong woman, a complete individual who lived her life on her own terms. And although we didn't get on sometimes – as you all know – she was always so funny.' Amelia is dressed in Sharon's tartan wrap, the one she wore at our Burns Supper the previous year in Coutal.

From all corners of the world, so many friends are with us in mind and spirit. In this echoing cathedral, at this moment, we mourn our loss, each surrounded by their own memories. My children, Irena and Ziggy, have lost their sparkling, exuberant aunt.

In her wicker coffin, Sharon lies anointed with Caudalie Huile Divine and Coutal lavender tucked under her pillow, wearing the kaftan Eunice made for her. Dougal, her trusty hairpiece, is woven into her hair.

Every year, I wrote out New Year's resolutions for both of us. Only when the final approval came, would they be typed up and displayed in a prominent position. I look at the list for 2015:

Sharon
- Finish bathrooms (or minimum one) by March
- Don't drink alcohol from Monday to Thursday up to end of March – then review position
- Exercise once a week
- Sort out boyfriend/dad material
- Job – go on a public speaking course, have more confidence
- Live more in the moment
- Create a medium-term (two-to-three-year) plan for living arrangements
- Concentrate on Will's happiness, e.g. find a school that suits and helps prepare him
- Plan a long-haul trip to support Amelia in her cycling charity event in India
- Go to Sicily at Easter
- Look after healthy relationships and get rid of those that aren't
- Alternate with Basia to have at least one big party every year

I compare this to the 2017 list:

Sharon
- Job – seek promotion, more income, more job satisfaction

- Job – seek job where I can work in London but live in Scotland
- Plan HOLIDAY for each school holiday
- Be receptive to idea of future relationship prospects. Consult trusted comrades before embarking
- Continue with public speaking course and building self-esteem
- Concentrate on Will's happiness, i.e. right school, right place
- Trial move to Scotland
- Do not let myself be bullied and follow my instincts
- Try and write diary. Keep my own counsel
- Chill more; fun things for me (no self-flagellation)

The following year, all the resolutions had been met and surpassed. There was only one word for the 2020 resolution list: "Survive".

The cathedral Covid bouncers bar Susan's entry into the cathedral, and she leans by the wall outside, gently weeping.

The crematorium is more restful. Naomi, Sharon's youngest sister, shuffles her chair beside her husband and sets off a flurry of shuffling, as we all move next to our own. Holding hands, we grip onto some solace in a sea of grief. The piper strikes up "Amazing Grace" and "The Skye Boat Song" and then the finale, the beautiful rendering of the tune "Panis angelicus", one of the many songs Sharon used to sing to herself throughout the day, sotto voce.

The funeral is the nightmare that keeps on giving. We chat outside to the others and pass around a bottle. One mourner turns to me and says, 'I didn't like you at the beginning, but I've warmed to you.'

Christ! Like Father Jack on Craggy Island, this is turning into another *Father Ted* scenario. *Drink* is the only solution!

An old friend of Sharon's comes up to me shortly afterwards and says: 'She always loved you; I remember her saying how kind you were, especially when Will was born.' I look at her, uncomprehendingly. I can't work out if she is being patronising, or not. Certainly, my oversensitivity ensures that I feel diminished, inconsequential and marginalised. That isn't necessarily her fault. I keep reminding myself, how I feel is my responsibility. *I'll have to keep myself in check. Be nice*, I sternly tell myself.

'You know,' she carries on, 'you catered for her emotional side, whilst I catered for her intellectual side.' The plunging rapier, right between the shoulder blades.

'*Ram it, Bunty!*' I nearly blurt it out. Enough is enough, or as we say in France, *un oeuf, c'est un oeuf.* At least I am not monolingual. As we say in Glasgow, it's enough to give you the *boke*: the dry *boke*. It's enough to make you want to throw up.

Il y a des gifles qui manquent! In other words, someone has been totally out of order and deserves a slap but doesn't get one.

Sometimes, you just have to pick yourself up, toss back your hair and follow Dorothy Parker's dictum: "I get up in the morning, brush teeth and sharpen my tongue".

Sharon had destroyed the Gladstone mask. I still have my Churchill mask, ready to place in the barn walls in Coutal Haut. One day I will walk up the track and do this final act.

As Sharon would have said triumphantly, 'It had to be done and it *was* done!'

January & February 2021 *Outside World*

Who are we, trapped in our ways
Of dying towards the fact
Of only once having been, together
Or separate in our own being
But never wholly separate, only a part
Of the time we live in, and with others occupy

Poem from *Outside the Narrative*, Tom Leonard

The months have dragged on since Sharon died. Autumn has slipped away and now winter has come. Brexit has come to pass as one day we knew it would. Unsurprisingly, there are miles of lorries that stretch back from Dover into the Kent countryside. Now that we are outside the EU, all checks have taken longer. Perishable items perish. Fishermen are furious that they have been shafted, or rather, harpooned, and that there is a consequent ban on live seafood exports. We watch an item on TV and nod sympathetically when a distressed owner of an eel farm complains that he cannot sell his produce to the European markets anymore. The screen pans into a basin full of lively elvers. Then he adds that he voted for Brexit. Our sympathy vanishes. One of our neighbours, Chas, who has had a house in France for the last thirty years, writes of the expense, travel and bureaucratic nightmare in trying to obtain a visa. This is merely the beginning. Another neighbour, Bill, sends on an email from his brother who imports antiques from France to Britain.

His brother had recently engaged a transporter to pick up a load of furniture, rather than transport it himself, due to the appalling lack of information from the government. His transporter wrote in frustration:

> *What a f****ng nightmare, constant emailing, phone calls, texts back and forth to my clearing agent, chasing missing or incorrect information from French vendors, eventually told all looks good to present to customs and get clearance.... but customs are now closed and won't be open until Monday, so it's another forty-eight hours on top of the forty-eight since the fairs finished. In a truck stop with no dining facilities and nowhere close by to eat. Thank you f****ng Brexshit.*

There is a domino fold of businesses.

It looks like the prediction of Sir Martin Donnelly (former Permanent Secretary at the Department for International Trade) on the dangers of Brexit is becoming reality: 'You're giving up a three-course meal... for the promise of a packet of crisps...'

As Covid reasserts its grip, France announces that it is

closing its borders with all countries except to those in the EU. We are truly now out in the cold. Quarantine hotels have been designated for those who fly into Britain, charging £1700 for a ten-day stay, on a par with similar measures in the rest of Europe. When I hear of selfish people zipping around the UK, I burn with anger. There are too many who have made sacrifices, too many who have suffered. There is a school of thought that "only the little people abide by Covid rules", which is reminiscent of the famous line by the American businesswoman, Leona Helmsley, also known as "Queen of Mean", who was found guilty of tax evasion: "We don't pay taxes. Only the little people pay taxes".

It seems that the UK is now the furthermost outpost of the USA, the moon notwithstanding. Covid and Brexit have been eclipsed by a modern American catastrophe. For a long time, Gerry has been bemused by the increasingly unhinged tweets of Donald Trump, which have not been reported in the news. My favourite tweet is the dismissal of Joe Biden, refusing categorically to recognise him as the winner of the election. It simply said: *Bye den*. The clip of Trump's "spiritual advisor", her voice rising to a crescendo, '*Aka! Aka! Aka!*' as she invokes the spirits to come to the aid of the Great Leader. It is truly bonkers. Strange to think he has a spiritual advisor. Trump's retinue bolster the hysteria, as they all make equally outlandish claims to justify their assertion that the election has been stolen from them. Apparently, the Chinese and the Russians were involved; dead people in Nevada had voted, even Hugo Chávez had risen from his Venezuelan grave to spread the spectre of Communism; infiltrators, conspiracy theories and traitors lurked round every corner. Rudy Giuliani, erstwhile mayor of New York and Trump's consigliere, held a press conference on an industrial site between a porn shop and a crematorium (his team thought they had booked the Four Seasons hotel and not the landscape company of the same name), and two weeks later, Giuliani was filmed with black hair dye running down the crevices of his cheeks. Unpalatable though his politics may be, it felt refreshing to find a politician saying exactly what he meant. One quote by Trump sticks in my mind… "It's not as if America is that good either…". Pulling out of Middle East wars fabricated by lies and deception (there were no weapons of mass destruction lurking in Iraq) struck a chord with many. After all, war is all about power and commerce.

As Melania Trump was busy rearranging the ceramics for a photo shoot in the White House, Trump himself busied himself whipping up the crowd. 'You'll never take back our country by weakness; you have to show strength, and you have to be strong,' as his slavish supporters marched on the Capitol. They sauntered into the hallowed institution and took selfies with gorilla guy and some bikers from Nowheresville. There was no evidence of tear gas or heavily armed police. After all, this was not a Black Lives Matter matter.

The second attempt to impeach Trump has been unsuccessful, despite the lurid visual evidence clearly showing how close the politicians in the senate were to being killed. No one has yet answered the question: why did it take so many hours for the National Guard to turn up?

Covid cases in the UK have surged well into six figures, but now that the mass vaccination programme has been rolled out, Boris Johnson can breathe a sigh of relief. There is a palpable sense of hope… not just one vaccine, developed in a UK lab, but two! Buoyed by the swing of fortunes and in order to whip up support for the Unionist cause, Boris whizzes up for a day in Scotland to show his face as our own Great Leader. This is much to the consternation of Nicola Sturgeon, who suggests that maybe it's better to heed his own advice and *stay at home*. This provokes the lounge lizard, Jacob Rees-Mogg, MP, to mock her as "Mrs Moanalot", and add that the Scots should be grateful that the great British Army has risen to the challenge to roll out the vaccine in Scotland. This prompts the reply that the Scots also pay for the army. It is not a successful visitation. Boris dons a lab coat, keeps well away from the public ('tis, after all, a pandemic) and dutifully squirts the vaccine into a few phials for a photo shoot, which is ruined when the suction *sooked* it back up the syringe. Gerry remarks that a friend from Castlemilk, *Château du lait*, on the outskirts of Glasgow, his neck of the woods, told him that Johnson turned up with a posse of police, met not one local, bumped elbows with the troops in the vaccination centre, then popped off after ten minutes.

The whole atmosphere of disenchantment and cynicism is summed up neatly in a series of tweets by a diplomat (who has since resigned), Alexandra Hall Hall:

> *I woke up this morning feeling strangely unsettled… and realised that despite (or perhaps, because of) 30 +yrs in conventional govt service, I'm now starting to question everything I thought I once knew about my country and its institutions.*
>
> *Top down, our system is undemocratic – prerogative powers exercised on behalf of the Crown, unelected House of Lords, system that gives disproportionate powers to govt, elected with less than 50% vote, imbalance in powers across the Union, cozy nexus of donors, media, politicians.*
>
> *Populace kept distracted and entertained with never-ending diet of shallow news and gossip about royals, toffs, socialites, models, sports, pop, soaps, crime, etc. Feel-good stories or trivia which gloss over the challenges and inequities which actually prevail in our society.*

*But getting so much worse under this govt, with its systematic
efforts to attack and undermine any institutions which counter
its narrative or try to hold it to account – parl't, judiciary, NGOs,
human rights experts, investigative journalists, standards watchdogs,
liberals, etc.*

*And most sickening of all, shameless posturing and co-option
of supposed 'patriotic' icons – flags, Churchill, WW2, Britannia, the
monarchy, the army, Spirit of the Blitz, pint glasses, and invented
rows with external so-called enemies – the French, the EU, the Irish.*

*Ignoring real threats confronting us – internal and external.
Incompetent, self-serving govt at home, failing to tackle domestic
challenges; posturing on global issues and our values overseas, while
accepting dirty money, selling arms to dubious regimes, and cutting
aid.*

Alexandra Hall Hall. Twitter thread. 7 January 2022

***

The message *stay at home* has not quite sunk in. Prince
William and his wife take a trip up in the royal train to say
thanks to NHS workers then pop back to London, and Prince
Edward is mooted as being flown in to take up residence as
a full-time royal in Scotland. Who cares now, given that the
pandemic has mutated, and the economy is on its knees?
Nicola Sturgeon keeps reminding us about the FACTS
mantra, which, as a nation, we find it difficult to remember,
let alone adhere to: Face coverings, Avoid everyone, Clean
your hands, Two metres apart, Self-isolate if you feel sick,
then get a test. I think that's it. After the on-off-on-off kerfuffle
about Christmas (lockdown or no lockdown?), I read about
a perfect solution: "Here's what we can do about Christmas.
Why not open up all schools and allow family gatherings to
take place there? According to government advice, people

from up to thirty-three different households could meet up in each classroom in perfect safety, without any social distancing required whatsoever".

The year 2021 has started in Lockdown Two. Hogmanay is heralded with some rogue fireworks and covert gatherings outside. Besides that, revelry has moved to another planet. I have been dreading going back to work as a schoolteacher on 6 January. The TV screens show science classrooms with pupils masked and socially distanced by two metres. That has not been my experience. To be told that there is nothing to worry about being stuck in a room with twenty-five to thirty-three different young adults, with classes changing every fifty minutes throughout the school day is not reassuring, especially if you can't meet more than one person outside from a distance. It's a psychological head mincer. To assume that teenagers are biddable, compliant creatures and not bursting with hormones and desperate to jump on each other, is to be blind and unaware. Our Council Leader of Education announces: 'You don't come to Glasgow for an easy shift.' I concur, as I shift uneasily. Gerry has been given the *jag* early as an NHS employee. I will have to be patient.

Schools in England are open for a day to encourage the virus to circulate before being promptly shut down again. I am relieved when the schools in Scotland don't open at all on the prescribed date and we work online from home, as we did in the first lockdown. We have to up our game and master new technical skills and navigate a different way of learning. Closing schools is the right decision. In any case, it is the fastest commute I have ever had: a slide down the banister, then plonk into the chair, in front of the computer screen. In France, though, schools are open.

Captain Sir Tom Moore, the national hero latched onto by

the press and public alike, has died of Covid at the tender age of one hundred. He won acclaim after completing one hundred laps of his garden to raise nearly £33 million in charitable donations for the NHS. Is it uncharitable of me to suggest that the health service should not rely on charity, that instead people should pay more in taxes to keep it going? If this is an institution to treasure, then we should stop the government from selling it off to private companies. The American system of private health insurance has proved itself woefully inept at serving its citizens during a pandemic. Bernie Sanders, the former US presidential candidate, highlighted the fact that a phial of insulin in the US costs ten times more than it costs in Canada.

The healthcare system in France (a mix of private and public) is funded by health insurance contributions (*sécurité sociale*) which are deducted from workers' salaries, with employers contributing the lion's share. What is striking, is that the French system offers a high level of preventative healthcare. Available services include addiction prevention, regular medical check-ups and the promotion of physical activity and healthy eating. It is no surprise then, that the French pride themselves on a first-class medical service and French women have the second-highest life expectancy in the world. The UK is not even in the top ten.

Is it cynical of me to point out that Captain Moore, who seemed like a good, honourable man, is a Conservative party publicist's dream? He has been used to form an idea of "Great British pluck and fortitude", much like his female counterpart, Vera Lynn, who died the previous year at the age of 103. We have been exhorted again, to come out for "The Big Clap" on Thursday evening to remember the captain and his deeds. I am sure that the captain would not have wanted to be politicised, his achievement used as part of governmental spin. I can imagine Boris sitting on his Union Jack armchair with a piece of paper and a pencil stub. 'Two vaccines, *tick*; R number steadying, *tick*; honour the memory of dear Cap'n Tom, *tick*… now what's the next thing? Oh yes, Scotland would be nothing without us, better let these pesky Scots know super quick.'

Gerry and I watched a documentary written by the broadcaster Lesley Riddoch, called *Estonia – The Rise of the Baltic Tiger*. Riddoch had tried to get the BBC to commission it, but they refused, saying, "it is not for us". Unsurprisingly, it reveals that small countries can do well on their own. Small can be beautiful. Estonia is tiny, about the size of Wales, with a population of 1.3 million. Few thought it could survive independently. In thirty years, the Baltic Republic was transformed from a Soviet backwater into Europe's digital powerhouse. What is remarkable is that it broke free from its Soviet overlord in a bloodless, peaceful revolution. There is a lovely image of a two-million-strong human chain on one day in August, stretching from Tallinn to Vilnius. This, as a show of solidarity from the people of Lithuania, Latvia and Estonia. Previously, the Soviet Union was its only trading partner, so overnight, they lost all their trade. All rouble pensions were wiped out as the rouble was dumped and the new currency was pegged to the Deutsch mark. Estonia has hardly any natural resources, so the future did indeed look bleak. However, the Estonians realised that where they were on a level playing-field with the rest of the world was in relation to the world wide web, still in its infancy. Children were educated to be digitally literate from nursery stage, with computers placed in every nursery and school. Today, almost every school delivers its entire curriculum using digital technology. This helped Estonians take a relatively short-lived Covid lockdown in their stride and decide to scrap all external exams until the final years of school. It's a novel approach that's produced digitally savvy, entrepreneurial youngsters, such as the brains behind international success stories like Skype and Bolt. The flat income tax rate of 20% was controversial. However, it has attracted a lot of European investment and Estonia has turned its outlook firmly to the West, rather than the East. The apron strings of the former Soviet Union have been truly cut. Nonetheless, the total digital dependency appears to me, to be very state-controlled, as each citizen has an e-ID card with all personal information stored online. It takes about one minute to declare taxes and sign documents online using digital signatures. This has already saved 2% of GDP.

Our Estonian friend, Jan, who came to live in Scotland, described feeling a kindred spirit here with his homeland. He put it to us like this: 'Yes, of course it was very difficult at the beginning, there were a lot of problems. But it was an exciting time, and it is a very youthful population. Everyone wanted this to work. Scotland can do the same. As for you, thinking that we are all digitally tagged, it is simply not true. It's in our power to find out to what the state has on us e.g. speeding fines etc! As it is frequently pointed out, no independent country has ever demanded that it go back in time and tie itself to its former partner'.

The thought of this great leap forward is both frightening and exhilarating. Scotland needs to be back in the bosom of Europe. The media campaign telling us how we are too small, too stupid, too ineffectual and can't even speak the Queen's English has started to ramp up. This will no doubt reach a crescendo in time for the Scottish elections in May 2022. These will decide if a referendum for Scotland to split up from the rest of the UK is on the cards. A policy unit has been set up by the Westminster government to ensure the continuity of the Union, but within a matter of weeks, two leaders of the unit resigned. Cracks are appearing in this United Kingdom at an alarming rate.

***

The recent success in court by Uber drivers demanding that they, in the future, will have the same statutory rights as other workers in terms of sick pay, breaks and holidays and the right to belong to a trade union, has also exposed the con of the gig economy. It cannot flourish in times of a pandemic. Surely, at the end of this, we will see greater divisions in society between the haves and the have-nots.

My daughter Irena worked a few stints as a waitress in a champagne bar in town when she was a student. Granted, this is casual work, but more than once she was called in for a shift, only to be told after an hour that it was too quiet and, therefore, she was sent home. One snowy December evening, she was called into work. I protested, 'But it's my birthday, and I've organised a dinner.' Irena tearfully replied that if she refused, they would not give her the Christmas shifts, which was the time when the public tipped generously. A welcome boost to their minimum wage. She dutifully arrived at the bar, only to find that the snow had stopped most people from going out and so she was sent home again.

'But the buses aren't running – could you help to pay for a taxi for me?' she asked her boss. 'No,' was the brisk answer. It took her three hours to get home, after at last catching one of the few taxis around. She had to pay out double what she had earned that evening. Ken Loach's film, *Sorry We Missed You* (as well as *I, Daniel Blake*) should be made compulsory viewing in secondary schools, showing the tribulations of a delivery driver who had the same experience as others, such as Uber drivers, in the gig economy.

In Texas, the storms and arctic conditions have caused mayhem, as has Senator Ted Cruz, who snuck off to Cancun from his home in Texas for a sunny holiday with his family, leaving his constituents to battle it out for themselves. When this was discovered, he blamed his daughters. Worse was to come when it was discovered that the family had left their poodle, Snowflake, at home, alone, staring balefully out of the window.

"Small can be beautiful", as Gerry tells me frequently. Govanhill is a sliver of a place, a poor area in the south side of Glasgow, which has historically been the landing stage of many asylum seekers and immigrants. There are eighty-eight languages spoken here, and it was curiosity, and a dod of vanity, that prompted me to tune into their week-long Bhasha Glasgow Language Festival at the end of February. Having no expectations, I was pleasantly surprised, how even a virtual event can be moving and spontaneous, as a recitation of a Polish poem extolling the joys of mushroom picking in Polish forests was enhanced by the sound of a dog barking in the background in time to the cadences of the poem.

***

Apart from the vaccines spreading their magic, the only other piece of wonderful news is the landing of the Perseverance Rover, three hundred million miles away on Mars. Rather like a Tonka Toy Truck with appealing gizmos, such as a helicopter. All the technology sends the first pictures of the red planet back to Earth. Mars is becoming a popular destination; China and Russia's spacecraft will follow shortly behind. Even the United Arab Emirates have joined the party with a spacecraft circling Mars.

Truly a terrific distance away.

I believe that those naming the Rovers are closet wine connoisseurs, as the previous space invaders were called "Spirit", "Opportunity", and "Curiosity". This prompted a happy Saturday morning perusing NASA's site and realising that I too, could sign up to sending my name to Mars on the next mission and could acquire a boarding pass and frequent flyer status. I note that there are five million other humans already signed up. Holidays on dreary Earth could be old hat! It's already too full, too polluted, too wasted and too disease-ridden. Mars might be minus sixty-three degrees centigrade with a teeny bit of oxygen, but it would be the holiday of a lifetime, seeking signs of ancient life.

As we marvel at this (remote) possibility, a real-life Earth experience hits the outer atmosphere; plumes of smoke and belching fire erupt from Mount Etna. It is a spectacular show, as ash rains down on the surrounding towns. How we wish we were back in Sicily, sitting on a terrace sipping cocktails in Taormina with Sharon, Fran and Will (a mocktail for the latter), watching this theatrical performance. Mars will have to wait.

Out of the Gloaming

Dreich weather is on the cards in this northern outpost for the tail end of February. 'Sorry to tell you this,' say our friends in France unapologetically, 'but it's lovely and sunny here, hovering around nineteen degrees. Springtime!'

The Scottish winter is easy for us; one flick of a switch and the central heating comes on. Not for us, the scurrying into the house with a big pile of logs that is greedily consumed by the fire. This had been our experience the previous two winters in France, our clothes constantly redolent of wood smoke.

Very little is said about France or indeed the rest of Europe; nothing about the flooding in Southwest France. Friends tell us that a small stream is running down our track from the house. Our garage has been broken into, even though there is very little to steal from us. We have lent our French car out to neighbours, Jill and Simon. They are going to park it outside our house from now on and move it around every so often to give a semblance that someone is home. We should put up a sign in French to indicate that there are better pickings elsewhere. *C'est mieux ailleurs.* 'To be honest,' says Linda, 'this winter has been very much like last winter; quieter, maybe, not much going on.' Lot-et-Garonne has reverted into a sleepy backwater.

We watch Rick Stein's culinary tour of France on TV and are filled with nostalgia. 'Look, he's in the same restaurant in Périgueux that we went to with Jo and Grant! Not far from the *Heilin Coo.*' The chef was evidently following the same itinerary as we had when he rolled up in the picture-perfect village of Trémolat. What I did not know was that the village provided the setting for the famous Chabrol film, *Le Boucher.* It's no spoiler to say that the butcher is the killer. I remember having nightmares after watching the film years ago. Lately, we have watched reams of French series: *Call My Agent, Engrenages* (*Spiral*), *Lupin, Plan Coeur.*

Today, Gerry has announced in all seriousness, 'We need to buy a bigger television.' I argue that we have had the TV for at least ten years and there is nothing wrong with it. I think this is called "pent-up spending". The Sunday papers still contain "Travel Sections" – places you can aspire to visit when all this is over.

Rocco the Labrador has just turned nine years old and is in tip-top condition, albeit with a smattering of white hair under his chin. He still drools at the sight of a carrot. The pandemic has brought him a slew of gorgeous students from the "BorrowMyDoggy" scheme, desperate to have an excuse to go on long, long walks to break the monotony of lockdown. I thought they may have melted away when I texted them to ask if they wanted to take him for a walk the following week. Except I didn't. I had asked them if they would like to take the boy out for a wank. Fat fingers or predictive text? There were no takers. Oh, that all important one letter. Rocco's humans wait on him hand and foot and he deigns to let us rub his neck and tummy every morning. Strangely enough, Rocco has reverted to being a playful pup again and expects us to play with one of his many chewed-up toys on return from his promenade: Bananaman, Waggy, Piggy, Toucy, Monkey, Crabby, Ducky and Chicken. Owning a dog is now de rigueur and dognapping is on the increase. I try to guess at the breed of dogs walking on the path in front of our house and note the rise in popularity of mixed breeds such as Cockerpoos, Cavapoos and Labradoodles, as well as mixes with Huskies called, perhaps, Cockerhusks and Huskeypoos. It's a weird dog world out there. As the famous dog philosopher, Iggy Pop, once said, "be the person your dog thinks you are".

***

Our next-door neighbours here in Glasgow, Jen and Fran, have been my friends since childhood. By good fortune, we have lived in consecutive houses that overlook the canal for the last few years. We call ourselves "The Schemies" and look out for each other. They both visited Coutal the year we were renovating the house. Back in Scotland, we look outside onto the water of the canal, enjoy the wildlife and make sure our swans are fed. Jen has bought swan food and is down by the quayside every morning. As the temperatures plummet and the city is transformed into a winter wonderland, our lockdown cage has now been reinforced by arctic conditions. We worry that we have not seen our swans for a few days. Jen texts with a photo of the swans hungrily pecking away at their breakfast. *They were waddling ungainly across the ice to their compliant humans. We'd walk a million miles...* No doubt they have been imbibing the dregs of the Buckie bottles (Buckfast – the choice tipple of the drunks in these parts) that skeeter on the ice.

It has been nearly a year since the first lockdown happened. To keep himself busy, Gerry painted the whole house, correctly reasoning that we were going nowhere fast. Nearly a year later, we get round to hanging the pictures back on the wall. I am trying to get into a new regime, practising yoga and cutting down on the calories. So far, yoga, one, calorie reduction, nil. Apparently, a banana has 108 calories, and a gin & tonic has ninety-one calories. Gerry has been ensconced on the sofa with a beer or five watching the rugby season unfold. So far, Scotland has managed to snatch defeat from the jaws of success. As the famous philosopher, José Mourinho, once commented (albeit on Andy Murray's defeat to Roger Federer): 'Sometimes a big defeat is the start of many victories.'

I watch the neighbour across the road, a PE teacher, doing his squats and leg thrusts with a pulley system on the deck then going indoors to do another few hundred cycles on his stationary bike in his living room. Runners in shorts with lobster legs tear round the canal path, as if mocking me. I mentally take note that self-control and restraint are required. Thoughts meander in my head, as my body grinds to a halt.

The snowfall has produced the best skiing conditions ever, here in Scotland. Yet no one is allowed to venture to the ski slopes. Rather like the shipping forecast, we are entertained by the names bestowed on the gritters or snowploughs: Gritty Gritty Bang Bang, Yes Sir Ice Can Boogie, Chilly Connolly, Darth Spreader, For Your Ice Only, Gritney Speirs, I Want to Break Freeze, Grit Expectations, Gritter Thunberg, Spready Mercury, Sir Andy Flurry, Slippy McGritty and my absolute favourite, Slushily Distanced.

Five

The Forth & Clyde Canal *Pulsating*

'I love the name of the place where you live,' says Josette, a French friend. I look at her sceptically. 'You are joking, right? Ruchill? Are you having a laugh?' It sounds too guttural.

'You are not pronouncing it correctly,' she corrects me, 'Roosheel.'

'*Bien sûr*,' I counter, 'just on the border of *La Colline de Marie* – Maryhill.' From our house, we note all the teeming wildlife on the canal. As well as the swans, there have been sightings of moorhens, ducks, cormorants, kingfishers, herons and otters. One misty winter morning, a friend was cycling to work along the canal path, when suddenly, imperceptibly through the haar, he saw something that looked like a tree moving across the canal. It came closer and closer and, as it emerged, he realised it was a stag with huge antlers swimming from one bank to the other. He set the record for wildlife sightings on his commute to work that morning! Our view through the bare winter trees reveals the dramatic sweep of the bend of the canal. The University of Glasgow tower, the Campsie Fells, the Gleniffer Braes and the wind turbines dot the horizon. Or, if I were an estate agent, our view "boasts a sublime cityscape".

The cleaning up of the Forth and Clyde Canal was a Millennium Project; at one point, there had been talk of it being filled in, since its use was obsolete, and it was deemed a public danger. It was even suggested that a motorway be built in its place. I recall walking down the overgrown pathway years ago; the green, putrid phosphorus and stinking slime would surely have swallowed up any poor soul or animal who had the misfortune of falling in. Warning signs abounded.

And now, The Schemies – Gerry, me, Fran and Jen – are inveterate twitchers, reporting back on any unusual activity. Jen is particularly besotted by our swan couple, who fascinate us with their behaviour. We suspect that they are building a nest across from us on the banks of the canal. Jen even has swan slippers; not made out of actual swans, I hasten to add. All of us have been incarcerated. Working from home, mostly. The swans' pirouettes and antics are our sole entertainment. We envy them their freedom, swanning around. We decide not to give them names like "Swanny McSwanface" and "Gloria Swanson". They are, after all, wild animals; who knows what goes on in the head of a swan? Every day they wait for us at mealtimes, by the quayside (what we term a lump of concrete at the bottom of the slope). Jen has spoilt them by ordering special swan food because they have been sniffy about their food and leave the lettuce (not Romaine) and carrots, which are then snaffled by the ever-watchful cats and other birds. 'Did you see those people giving them bread? Completely lacking in nutrition!' snarls Jen. The swans are gradually becoming accustomed to their humans and allow us to approach them. So near, we can see deep into their black eyes. The cob is bigger, with a distinct proboscis above the middle of his eyes and is by far the bolder creature. Whenever he sees his humans – who he knows will be bringing vital deliveries of victuals – he steams ahead towards us. The pen is smaller, shyer and tends to hold back. They no longer bother hissing at us, but we have not been brave enough to proffer them food from our hands, not wishing to risk a sharp peck on the palm. There are other swan couples on the canal, all bigger than our own adopted couple, and they have marked out their territories. There do not seem to be any swan social gatherings; maybe they are socially distancing. Do swans ever get bored? Do they *hurrumph* like Rocco, waiting for excitement to be provided?

Our avian fascination, and the dearth of anything to do, provokes a to-ing and fro-ing of daily texts:

Jen:	*I see all the wee birds are "flocking" to your feeder, Fran*
Gerry:	*Flapping frenzy at Fran's full feeder*
Fran:	*This tiny blue tit swooped in for a sunflower seed but flew away with massive pizza crust*
Jen:	*The blackies looking for bruised fruit and cores. One of the few fruits the big bully boys don't seem to eat*
Gerry:	*Were they tweeting about it?*
Jen:	*Thrushes seem to be fond of a bit of fruit too. Formed a wee gang*
Gerry:	*Thrushes raisin their standards*
Jen:	*They don't give a fig!*
Gerry:	*They do when the wee bugger steals their fruit – robin bastard!*

Basia:	*Plumbing the depths here!*
Jen:	*Just ordered more duck and swan floating food with sunflower hearts*
Gerry:	*I had to wipe the snow off the mealworms this morning so the birds can see them*
Fran:	*The blue tits just love your worms*
Gerry:	*Just blue because of the cold weather... oooh matron!*
Jen:	*Just put food out for the swannies but my timing was off as they had just started their ritual coitus interruptus. So, I stood there feeling like a voyeur and ended up leaving food out. They have totally ignored it and gone over to their nest!*
Fran:	*Awe, the lovebirds!*
Basia:	*Voyeuse Gordon here swan-watching. Do you think they will stay across there – rather too small for a nest?*
Jen:	*Don't know. Too close to canal path*
Fran:	*They'll never be able to house their weans in that wee spot*
Jen:	*Probably just a wee resting spot for the day as they await their deliveries*
Basia:	*Let's build a coracle for them!*

It is telling that in lockdown, the world has slowed down, paradoxically all the impositions to our freedoms have made us more contemplative, more appreciative of each other and gentle pleasures. We have stopped the world; we have not fallen off. And so, with the absence of so many distractions, our minds are inordinately focused on swans and their habits.

Swans have been revered in the animal world for millennia. As well as beautiful, they are intelligent and firing on all senses. There is a myth that the human soul flies on in the swan after death.

There is something other-worldly about our swans. During the recent cold spell, the canal started to defrost, and a residue of water skimmed on the top; our "Jesus" swans looked as if they were walking on water and their reflection shimmered on the ice.

Swans must be top of the majesty rung, truly posh birds. This assumption takes a bit of knocking when I discover that a gathering of swans is called a "bevy of swans". No truer description for our swans in our canal, where there is every chance of them bumping into a bottle of Buckie whilst on their swan manoeuvres. Maybe ours should be called a "swally of swans", which rather knocks them off their pedestal.

The swans bob their heads upside down, kick up their legs, and their long necks stretch deep into the undergrowth. Sometimes they fan their wings and flap over the surface of the water for a short while. Swan exercises. Stretching themselves. Lately, they have been in full mating mode, in a balletic climax where two long necks twist together, like the union of two question marks. During the winter wonderland, where all was frozen, but the sun shone brightly, the searing whiteness of the swans and pristine white landscape blinded us. The swans are the ultimate cliché: regal, dignified, graceful, beautiful and so utterly disdainful. Rocco knows to keep far away from them. The swan incident has imprinted itself in his dog memory. In the glorious weather during Lockdown One of May last year, a swan couple had made their nest on the canal banks near the Firhill football stadium. I would take frequent walks with Rocco to check on their progress, as did many others. A walk with a purpose to the swan shrine. One visitor was a nursery schoolteacher who was busy filming the swans' progress and sending the clips back to her own housebound chicks. We were all eagerly waiting for them to hatch, and the pen was sitting proudly on her clutch of eggs – six in all. More and more people turned up nearer hatching day. One day, Rocco strayed too near to see what was going on and – understandably – one of the swans took a left swing with his/her beak, terrifying Rocco, who bolted with me – foolishly – hanging on to his lead. Eventually, I let go of the lead when it cut through my hand and watched Rocco disappear into the horizon. Hours later, I found my poor dog cowering in the wasteland.

A miracle – all but one of the eggs hatch. I watch as the cygnets emerge. It does not take long, a few days, for them to follow their parents into the water. One cygnet holds back, fearful, then his mother bumps him/her into the water with her beak. Swimming is second nature; it *is* nature, and the swan family entertain us all in their frequent outings.

I love our swans in Glasgow in the same way that I hate the ducks at the back of our house in France. That is so unfair; I am sorry for the ducks who live such an unnatural life waiting to be slaughtered. I am aware that I am a complete hypocrite, because I love eating duck!

Jen has just broken the "Sacred Order of Schemiedom" by buying a small ground-floor flat not far away. 'It's my knees,' she explains, 'it does them in going up and down a three-storey house.' Such a pathetic excuse to go upmarket to the West End.

We tease her. 'Do you think it will be all hoity-toity birds in your new place, peacocks and birds of paradise?' Nevertheless, I sympathise. My right knee creaks and grinds as I walk down the stairs. I quite understand what Jen means. Fewer stairs, fitter knees. We agree to extend the boundaries of the Schemiedom, but this is an exception to the rule. We solemnly toast the new estate order by drinking champagne over the bins outside, which keeps us "socially distanced"!

The kayakers have come out in the morning again,

soundlessly slicing through the water, but there is no trace of the barges. They will not be back for some time. A new bridge is being built as part of the beautification and gentrification scheme.

Most of the time, the swans and other wildlife have the canal to themselves. Nature is reclaiming its own. It was not always thus.

***

The Forth and Clyde Canal was built between 1768 and 1790 and is nearly forty miles long. It is an example of engineering brilliance, with thirty-nine locks as well as bascule bridges and aqueducts. Its raison d'être was to create a shortcut, linking the east to the west of the country, leading to the faster and more effective transportation of goods, essentially from the North Sea to the Atlantic. Thus, cutting out the long passage around the country; in effect a Scottish Suez Canal. It also connected the two main cities of Edinburgh and Glasgow. At the time it was built, it was a way for travellers to move around using "swift" boats which would link up with coach services. At the time, most people travelled from Leith, the port outside Edinburgh, to London by ship, rather than take the longer, more perilous land journey.

The chief engineer of this monumental project was called John Smeaton. Imagine – John Smeaton! The very name of the baggage hero who, in 2007, thwarted would-be terrorists in Glasgow Airport. He had been outside the main terminal building on a cigarette break, when he saw two men in a burning jeep trying to bulldoze through the airport entrance. The car was full of highly flammable gas cylinders. The attack was foiled when Smeaton and others attacked the men, intuitively, with their bare hands. They dragged them out of the jeep and tackled them to the ground. John Smeaton's immortal words resounded through the globe via the internet and news media: 'Glasgow doesn't accept this. This is Glasgow; we'll set aboot ye.'

In 1707, the union of Scotland and England was forged, and it was, and is, an emerging relationship, fraught with many a cross word. Crucially, the union allowed Scotland to trade with England's vast colonial market across the world. This, coupled with the explosion of the industrial revolution, meant that the central belt (the area between Edinburgh and Glasgow) was a powerhouse of trade, wealth and influence. Glasgow was better placed than London to sail to the Americas and to benefit from the tobacco trade, cutting almost twenty days from the journey. European demand for Virginia leaf was insatiable. The French government gave Glasgow a monopoly over all tobacco imports to its overseas territories, which gave British coffers a substantial boost.

What is now glossed over but spoken more about in the wake of Black Lives Matter, is Glasgow's role in the slave trade. Goods such as cloth, copper and firearms left Britain to be exchanged for slaves in West Africa (an estimated 1.5 million people) who would then be shipped across the Atlantic to work in America and the West Indies. The tobacco, sugar and rum that the slaves produced would then be shipped back to Britain. Glasgow benefited considerably from the slave trade. Street names such as Virginia Street, Tobago Street and Jamaica Street are constant reminders of Glasgow's complicity.

Slavery was eventually abolished in Scotland in 1778, by a historic ruling of the Scottish courts. This was thirteen years before the construction of the Forth and Clyde Canal. Change was in the air since the historic landmarks of the French Revolution in 1789 and the start of the American War of Independence in 1775. Incidentally, the compensation given to slave owners for freeing their slaves – £17 billion in today's terms – was only fully repaid by the British Government in 2015. (This means that most taxpayers today have been paying off this debt!)

In the eighteenth century, the building of the canal was a way of consolidating trade and the commercial success (on the back of slavery). This was now a prosperous, populous city which had had a massive investment in infrastructure and a ready workforce. Glasgow was rewarded with the Industrial Revolution, which spewed all over the city for the next 150 years, assuring its wealth, growth, poverty, exploitation and urban pollution. "Let Glasgow Flourish" is the city's motto.

Curiously, the enigmatic rhyme on the Glasgow coat of arms is one that can only be described as depressing:

There's the tree that never grew,
There's the bird that never flew,
There's the fish that never swam,
There's the bell that never rang

Apparently, the symbols of the tree, bird, fish and bell are all associated with the life of St Mungo, the patron saint of Glasgow, reflecting moments of his early life.

The canal became a hive of industry, and along its banks, mills and factories flourished: paint and match factories, a couple of iron foundries, Ruchill Sawmill and a string of glass works where furnaces were kept going all day and night, seven days a week. Not far from the canal, Cassel's potassium cyanide and gold extracting works added to this cocktail of smog and pollutants.

Gerry's brother, Douglas, remembers ordering rubber gym mats for his work from the MacLellan rubber works which, possibly, was on the spot where our house is now.

As a birthday present, Gerry gave me a framed series of photographs of the factories and warehouses along the canal. 'But why did they get rid of all these warehouses and the factories, some of which had huge arched windows?' I asked Gerry. After all, they were prime examples of industrial architecture. And the answer came that it was impossible to "detox" the buildings, more poison than brown sites; an embryonic Chernobyl. It was far easier to pull them down and start afresh.

At the same time as the industrial frenzy took its toll, the canal also catered for the logs from the Baltic states which travelled east to the sawmill (this wood furnished the floors of the spacious West End tenement flats); cargo boats, barges, puffers and pleasure steamers – called *Fairy Queen*, *May Queen* and *Gypsy Queen* – took the locals on a mini *doon the watter* daytrip to a tearoom outside the village of Kilsyth, for an extremely rare break from the grind of their lives.

The canal in Maryhill was also the starting point for prisoners making their journey to the penal colonies of Botany Bay in Australia. For many who lived in Maryhill and Ruchill it was a brutal, short life full of hardship in a place where even the trees in Ruchill Park had to be strong to survive the putrid, noxious atmosphere. The local brewery did a roaring trade to the many pubs in the area, selling weak beer to the workers. It was no wonder that one of the first Temperance Societies was founded here, and no surprise that it failed utterly. Alcohol has been part of the social fabric here for centuries. Even children had a brutal life. In the UK, the 1833 Factory Act declared that the emergence of a second molar tooth (at approximately twelve years of age) was acceptable proof that a child was old enough to work.

I can conjure up in my head the poverty, cacophony, the clamour, the pulsating life, smells and colour of this canal.

I find the spur of the canal from the Kelvin Dock to Speirs Wharf fascinating. It was the final part of the canal to be completed, and what were formerly the City of Glasgow Grain Mills and Stores and the Forth and Clyde Navigation Company offices in Speirs Wharf, are now luxury flats with a residential spa. We regard this three-mile stretch as "our" part of the canal. Possibly because I was born nearby in a tenement in South Woodside Road. We commune with this stretch of the canal on a daily basis. It is only a forty-minute walk down the towpath to the city centre. Now, panels depicting local history are scattered around, detailing the sites and stories of the cinema, pubs, the tall ships, the visit of Roy Rogers and his horse, Trigger. They tell too of boats built in the Kelvin Dock which ended up in Normandy, where they landed Allied forces during the decisive D-Day invasion of Nazi-occupied France in 1944.

One panel that resonates is the public announcement of the outbreak of cholera in 1832. *Mon Dieu!* Pestilence again!

The importance of the canal waned as roads improved and railways criss-crossed the country. Heavy industry gradually declined, and the factories closed down, one by one. The canal was officially closed on 31 December 1962 and declined into a mire of weeds and discarded shopping trolleys. I was hardly aware of its proximity when I frequently visited my Auntie Margaret's antique shop on Maryhill Road. Nothing was done to encourage investment and development in what became a run-down part of town, with its overcrowded tenements in a maze of streets.

Glasgow's designation as "European Capital of Culture" in 1990 was a pivotal moment in the city's fortunes which reignited an interest in its glorious heritage. No longer would it be described as the 'rumbunctious underbelly of the North' (*The Lonely Planet* guide, circa 1975). Suddenly, the ugly duckling of Europe emerged into a swan, wings beating. The city was designated "Britain's City of Architecture and Design" in 1999. This sealed the city's long-overdue renaissance and rediscovered civic pride. Glasgow, after all, has the oldest museum in the world, dating back 330 million years, to a time when Scotland was located near the equator and the climate was hot, damp and steamy. Only the dampness has remained. The Fossil Grove houses eleven intact, well-preserved fossilised ancestors of today's trees from a carboniferous forest.

The Glasgow Subway, built in 1896, is the third oldest in the world, after London and Budapest. It has never expanded from its original fifteen stations. There seemed no need to, as Glasgow had an extensive tram network from 1894, with over a thousand trams. (Sadly, the tram system was closed in 1962.) The subway was very run-down and closed at the end of the 1970s for badly needed upgrading. When it eventually reopened a few years later, it was rebranded the "Clockwork Orange" by the media, due to its newly adopted vibrant orange colour, and the fact it just went round and round with an inner and outer line. A friend told me her mum was in the middle of serving dinner in their tenement flat when a familiar shudder rocked the building. 'Oh my God,' she screamed, 'it's back!' A metaphor for Glasgow.

Preserving the sandstone architecture, the subway and the canal at the eleventh hour is the hallmark of the city leaders.

The canal was reprieved at the end of the 1990s by a European-funded project, as part of Glasgow's regeneration. The factories were pulled down and an ambitious recovery programme instigated. Houses and flats which reflected an "Amsterdam style" of living were built on the canal banks. If it had been in London, these flats and houses would have been snapped up in a jiffy, but the timing of the housing crash in 2009 was inauspicious.

When I bought a small flat in Ruchill in 2010, with its deck on the canal side as large in size as the whole flat itself, it had been lying empty for a year. It had been a casualty of the 2007–9 worldwide financial crisis. It didn't help that there was still a certain wariness about buying property in an area which, until recently, had been known as rough, violent, drug- and drink-addled. Cobblestone roads, vestiges of empty factories and tracts of wasteland were telltale signs that complete gentrification had not yet kicked in. It is still classed as a site of social deprivation.

The outside of the new estate was painted in block colours in the style of the Dutch artist, Piet Mondrian. The "Biennial" in Liverpool in 2014, which featured the artist's work, gave us an excuse to buy up Mondrian tat to decorate the flat. Apropos, when we visited Liverpool for the exhibition, we discovered the room in our hotel had no window. Feeling decidedly claustrophobic, we trudged down to the reception to complain. 'Did you ask for a room with a window?' asked the receptionist, and no, we had not. 'Loooek,' she said, in a winning Liverpudlian accent, pointing to the long list of terms and conditions on the booking form, and, sure enough, one could pay extra for the privilege of outside illumination. We were truly *gobsmaquéd*.

The University of Glasgow student residential village (called Murano, a nod to the Venetian glass factory and a link to glassworks that used to be situated in the same spot) is a mere five minutes' walk away. The mercury hit minus twenty degrees Celsius during our first winter in Ruchill. The canal froze over, and the students spent their days whizzing sofas up and down on the ice, lying back and shrieking with joy, glugging booze. It captures the spirit of the place. Even today, in lockdown, their students can be heard carousing from afar, ensuring that they are keeping their germs firmly sloshing amongst themselves. During the first lockdown, they stuck

SOS signs in the windows. This suited the Murano complex well, because the façade does look like a prison.

Our first canal excursion was on a cycle trip with our Argentinian friend, Pablo. We cycled on the canal path to the point in Falkirk where it meets the Union Canal and thence to Edinburgh. A distance of about seventy miles in total. We weren't aware that a torch was necessary to navigate through the blackness of the Union Canal. Pushing our bikes, clinging to the walls of the canal, we could hear and feel rats scurrying around our feet. At the end of the canal tunnel stood a redundant billboard with big letters saying, "DON'T FORGET YOUR TORCH". We had been cycling like the clappers, because Pablo had to be home to view a football match featuring Argentina. However, he had to concede that it was better if he just returned home before we reached Edinburgh and put himself out of his football misery. Another stop was required to calm down Fran, who had phoned to report on finding one of her tortoises, coincidentally another Pablo. This Pablo had been missing for three weeks and now had a shattered shell. When Fran was pacified and her wailing reduced to sobs, she sent him off to the tortoise hospital in Cumbernauld. We continued our cycle ride to Edinburgh and decided that we had to return by train because steam was rising from our saddle-sore bottoms. After that, I stuck closer to our canal neighbourhood.

Bridget, our friend who lives in the genteel West End, commented: 'I love where you live but couldn't live there myself – you have to go through *stuff*.' I'm not too sure what she means. It is on the other side of the house, away from the canal, deeper into Ruchill that provides local colour and excitement. The shop signs say it all: Bammy Beverages and Dapper Dandies (barbers), Saracen Interiors. Gerry suggests we give a free bottle of Buckfast from Bammy Beverages to sell with my book.

The film cameras have been out in the last few weeks, apparently filming a murder mystery series. Much to the amusement of other friends who quip: 'Come on, two weeks to find a murder in Maryhill, it must be Upper Maryhill.'

I sniff. 'High Ruchill, actually, by the way.' Yvonne, my aunt, sends a photo of "Fanny Floss" with the innocent question, *Just thought they might sell it in your neck of the woods?*

On the other side of Maryhill Road, beside Ruchill Church Hall (designed by Charles Rennie Mackintosh), the early shoots of gentrification are cautiously being planted in the fabulously named Shakespeare Street and Hathaway Street. Upmarket is still across the road. There is an invisible border.

Watching the emergent canal life has been a source of joy. All the colours of spring and the blossoming of the trees lighten the heart, bringing out the brightly painted barges (with their jaunty names like *Angel's Share*) and the kayakers, along with the teeming wildlife. Ironically, both lockdowns have contributed to the canal's natural cleansing. Fishermen tell me there is now an abundant supply of pike, carp and even trout! The water looks clean, but I have never been tempted to swim in it, although there is a water sports facility further up the canal. There is something very appealing about living so near water. As Gerry, the ex-shipyard worker, can testify. I do tell him frequently that his ship launching days are over.

The new craze that has taken over since Lockdown One is magnet fishing. I thought at first that it was fishing for fish with magnets. These new heavy, specially made rods with magnet tips that cost around £180 are used to haul out anything metallic from the bottom of the canal: knives, coins, World War One and Two memorabilia, but of course the most common catch is a supermarket trolley. In the bright future of après-Covid, we look forward to the dredger coming back for a big clean-up.

A year after I bought the flat, ever on the lookout for

places to store the dross of my children who regard our home as a dumping ground for their accumulated possessions, I had been watching for signs of life in a house up the street. I had noticed in another cold snap that there had been no footprints in the snow towards the front door. Peering through the glass, I could just make out the fungi on the wall and see that bits of the ceiling had fallen through. *Perfect*, I thought. *And now to wait for the house to go on the market.* The previous owners had fled to Australia after returning their keys to the mortgage company. After a year of legal wrangling, the house was put onto the market. Yet again, people were reluctant to buy it because of the water damage. Just the bargain I had been waiting for. I was the successful bidder! It took four months to dry out the house and it was lucky we could live in the flat whilst vital repairs were carried out. Our fellow Schemies have since moved in next door. We can now tip the kayak into the water from our house-deck (a two-minute operation) and peacefully glide down the canal in a meditative reverie.

Rocco, our hound, is forever trying to swim in the canal. If only we would throw his ball in so that he could live up to his full title of Labrador Retriever. I am being lulled here into a feeling of gentility. Where has the edginess gone? Glasgow has still not shaken off its violent image from the past. Nevertheless, I am still surprised when I see people shudder when I tell them that I come from Glasgow. Often, they ask me if it is safe to walk around at night. The only answer is that it is as safe as anywhere else. In spite of this, we are still confronted by the snobbery of our fellow Glaswegians when we tell them where we live. 'Ruchill! Surely you want to say, North Kelvinside? Is it not Junkieland?'

In pre-Covid times, I was walking with Rocco on the towpath, and we could hear the chant rise from the stands of Ruchill

Stadium. 'There is only one *Ziggy Gordon*!' to the tune of "Guantanamera". Who would have thought that Ziggy, my son, would have a season playing football for the "Jags", AKA Partick Thistle? How handy that the stadium is a mere stone's throw away from the house. Serendipity: everything has fallen into place. Curiously, on a recent walk, I could see people sitting in the stadium. On closer inspection, they were cardboard cut-outs to give a semblance of a crowd. After a year of this, we are hungry for venues to open up.

The stone signpost outside the tenement marking kilometres from Bergerac is a strange omen forging a link between these two disparate places.

Our homes in Ruchill and Lot-et-Garonne have a pleasing authenticity. Not too manicured, both are a bit rough and ready around the edges.

Jen phones me one day when I'm at work. 'The police have cordoned off the canal in front of your house!' The body of a young man, who has been missing for the last two months, has resurfaced, having floated under the ice for quite a distance. On another occasion, I hear a gun going off and discover there has been a shooting nearby. It was a drug-related crime. A man is killed in his car at the traffic lights underneath the canal viaduct.

Iffy territory, indeed.

Linda texts from France: *It's blawn a hooley here, just to let you know*. The lines are blurring.

Six

March & April 2021 *Outside World*

In France, the third lockdown started on 16 March 2021, although it doesn't appear as draconian as the first one. Our friends in Aquitaine tell us that the *attestation*, the official form, has been reinstated. As has the curfew from 7pm to 6am. Nevertheless, up to ten people can meet up. The uptake of vaccines is slow, not helped by President Macron's comment in January that the AstraZeneca *jag* is quasi-ineffective on people older than sixty. Gerry believes that the reason for the push for the Pfizer vaccine over the AstraZeneca in France, is to do with the fact that the manufacturers of the latter decided that, as a humanitarian act, it was not going to materially profit from it. Hence, the share market price went down, whilst the opposite is true for Pfizer, and they happily plunged into a profit-making enterprise.

The state-sponsored television service in Britain does

not overly dwell on the rest of Europe. We are on a far-flung northern outpost in this damp archipelago. There is, however, a brief report on Nicolas Sarkozy, the former French president, who has been sentenced to jail for three years for bribing a judge. He has been languishing under house arrest in his luxurious home in the centre of Paris.

Scotland's rugby win over France, a nail-biting last minute victory, gives welcome sustenance, for the Scots, on the sports front. But what happened to the top stories of strikes, gilets jaunes and the reconfiguring of local government which we heard about when we lived in France?

Gerry is up with the lark, or rather, with the swans, and listens to *France Bleu Périgord* as he takes Rocco for a walk in the park. When he returns home, he tops up his daily news consumption by listening to the British state broadcaster with me over breakfast. 'Did you hear about Israel being taken to the International Court in The Hague?' he asks.

'Really?' I reply.

'*Non,*' is his emphatic response. 'Did you hear about David Cameron giving taxpayers' money to his cronies?'

'Really?' I ask.

Again, '*Non*. Do you think the young people know that they are stuffed because we have such poor employment laws and one of the poorest pensions in the developed world? Do you hear anything about Julien Assange, the torturing and silencing of a journalist for exposing the dirty tricks of government?' *This is sounding like a lecture, Gerry.* 'Did you hear about Boris Johnson (or rather, the taxpayer) paying for his "lover" to attend various junkets around the world?'

'Really?' I sigh.

'*Non et non!*'

***

When I phone up our friends in Aquitaine, their conversation is peppered with new words. A new Covid vocabulary has been introduced since we left France (not even two years ago), to the consternation of the *Académie Française*, the stuffy gatekeepers of the purity of the French language. The French language is notoriously slow to evolve and the *Académie* has been on high alert since 1635. Its role is to expel any pesky invaders, especially of the English variety.

The first thing they had to do was to recognise the gender of the pandemic. It is a feminine word – *la Covid -19* however the virus is masculine*: le coronavirus.*

A few favourites:

Le confinement	Lockdown
Le réconfinement	Lockdown again
Bon confinement	Have a good Lockdown
Le deconfinement	Lifting of Lockdown
Le télétravail	Working from home
Les gestes barriers	All the things you have to do to protect yourself and others from contracting the virus
Skypéro	A virtual version of the all-important *apéro*, the indispensable pre-dinner drink
Apérue	Fusion of *apéro* and *rue* (street). A reference to when all bars and restaurants were shut and only operating a "to go" service. People would then have to drink their *apéros* in the street.
La distanciation sociale	Social distancing

I didn't know what the word "furlough" was when it was first used; I thought it had something to do with horses. Was I thinking of fetlock? In French, furlough is translated as *le chômage technique* or *l'activité partielle*.

Notwithstanding, there should be a sigh of relief from the *Académie* as there is one word that has re-emerged from obscurity: *l'anosmie*, which means the loss of the sense of smell. One of the effects of *la Covid-19*, or should I say *le coronavirus*.

Sneaky Parisian restaurateurs and café owners have been luring prospective clients by taking advantage of the "walk your dog" rule, by popping dogs into a pop-up dog-friendly area in the vicinity. The owners are permitted to have a quick drink before retrieving their canines and marching onwards.

Léa, one of my fellow French teachers at school, tells me that it is rather a relief to be spared the duty of kissing most people as a form of greeting. All these little stresses; how many times? *Yuk, sweaty face… ah, someone else has arrived into the fold, here we go again…* I make a mental note to avoid group hugging and oversharing when all this is over.

If children are not at school, then parents cannot work (to their full capacity). So, in France as in Britain, it has become an imperative to keep open the gates of learning, virtually, if not always physically. In a nutshell: no school, means no work, means the economy crashes. This has had some surprising consequences, especially in France. Some parents have responded by homeschooling their children themselves on a permanent basis. This has led the French Government to propose legislation which will make this far more difficult in the future. Underpinning this, is the assertion that homeschooling has allowed families to avoid teaching the country's core principle of state secularism, *laïcité*, which harks back to the Revolution when it was decreed that religion had no part in the new order. This in turn has caused increased tension in French schools today, especially for the Muslim community, regarding the wearing of headscarves and religious observance in school. From constantly stating that closing schools is non-negotiable, Macron closes schools for the next four weeks and clamps down on travel around the country. There is a sense of Macron panicking as his popularity slips. In a bid to curry favour with the discontented masses, he announces the closure of the elite school, ENA, that has dished out heads of state since 1945. *Enarques*, as the school's graduates are known, are invariably associated with the term *pantouflage*, referring to the revolving door between the public and private sectors. Once out of post, these ministers invariably pick up lucrative opportunities in private industry. Thus, it ever was!

About 150,000 shops deemed non-essential are closed in this latest lockdown, but the chocolate shops remain open. How could the French survive without chocolate at Easter? Easter for us is a quiet day spent indoors watching *Life of Brian* on the TV, nothing like a good execution to finish you off.

French lingerie shop owners have got their knickers in a twist at not being deemed "essential" in the Covid shopping pecking order and are protesting. If chocolate bunnies are allowed, why not the full bunny attire?

Meanwhile, here in Scotland, Nicola Sturgeon has just been subjected to eight hours of questioning at the Committee scrutinising the Scottish Government's handling of harassment complaints. It was a masterly performance. It's a pity that there will never be a possibility of such consummate performers, Nicola Sturgeon and Alex Salmond, coming together again to form a powerful political match. They are both at the top of the game. His evidence, a few days before, was measured, calm and forensic in his detail. A friend commented, if only he had shown such statesmanlike qualities when he was First Minister, rather than the tomfoolery and avuncular stuff he was prone to. Politicians in Scotland are foaming at the mouth at breaches of the ministerial code, whilst this causes no such consternation in England where politicians blithely breach standards of conduct with gleeful abandon. The Scottish politician gives the impression of some throwback to puritanical stuffed shirts, in comparison to their Westminster counterparts. Before the parliament in Scotland is dissolved in preparation for the election on 6 May, one last Bill is passed on 26 March, which states that everyone who has not raised an objection will be automatically registered as an organ donor.

The UK taxpayer paid a substantial amount of money so that the home secretary, Priti Patel, didn't have to go to court to answer why she broke the ministerial code. Cronyism and corruption are rampant. A financially clued-up friend, Lorna, writes of the Track and Trace system: "This system cost £37 billion. It contacted 9.1 million people which is over £400k a trace. This amount of money could have bought everyone a new home, got them to self-isolate for a year, paid them a salary and supplied them with free groceries from Waitrose!". An aphorism comes to mind: "they couldn't organise a piss-up in a brewery". However, these politicians are really good at syphoning funds towards their cronies' companies.

Despite the UK having the highest death toll in Europe for Covid, the government has at least succeeded in rolling out a slick vaccine operation, which has an immediate effect of reinstating the previous cockiness.

Priti Patel, the home secretary, calls for the "right" sort of asylum seeker to step forward, preferably not from a rubber dinghy, while she derides Black Lives Matter and Extinction Rebellion supporters, claiming the latter are "eco-crusaders turned criminals". Ironically, the overall numbers of asylum seekers are down from last year. Given that flights are cancelled, the only way to get to Britain is by boat. Rishi Sunak, the chancellor, cuts aid to Yemen (and many other places) whilst still selling arms to Saudi Arabia to bomb Yemen. Furthermore, he outlines plans for Britain's new sophisticated use of cyber weaponry to "prepare us for the wars of the future". This proposal would mean increasing the number of nuclear warheads (most of them conveniently nestling on the Clyde) from 180 to 260, an increase of over forty per cent. Given that it is estimated that one hundred warheads are all that's required for Armageddon, it would appear to smack of overkill. Obviously, he prefers to have a few up his sleeve.

***

It's enough to send you back to the comforting wings of swans. The 'Swan-Watch' committee has been out with the binoculars. Two nests have appeared, equidistant from our quayside, perfectly visible from our windows. One is the siesta nest and the other, we surmise, must be the birthing nest. 'The swans seem really hungry,' observes Fran. 'At least one is eating for two, or maybe six.' Our suspicions are confirmed as one enormous egg reveals itself tucked under a swan. Apparently, one egg is dropped every other day, until there is a maximum of six eggs. Early April is the optimum time for eggs to be laid, so our swans are bang on time!

A container ship called the *Ever Given* becomes stuck in the Suez Canal. There is a tailback of hundreds of ships and boats and the loss of billions of dollars. We have our own Suez Canal stand-off on a micro scale. Fran has gone down to feed the swans and, as they are steaming towards her, four kayakers are caught in the crossfire. The swans are obviously rattled. Everything comes to a standstill for at least three minutes, when the kayakers veer to the edge and the swans make a beeline to the waiting banquet of sunflower hearts.

'Do you remember last April?' asks my friend Bridget. It was the beginning of the first lockdown and the weather was glorious. Everyone basking in the sun, even though we were not allowed to travel outside the confines of our allotted spaces. There was a holiday atmosphere, and the smell of barbecues permeated the air. This time round, one whole year later, we are desperate for Breakout. The hairdressers reopen on 5 April, but retailers won't open their doors until the 26th, and even then, only "if we are good".

***

Remembering.

There is a monument here in a park in Glasgow and, behind it, the Union Jack is at half-mast. The university tower looms over us; a pale sun hovers over this small, socially distanced gathering, heads bowed, remembering a massacre that happened seventy-three years ago, in a place far away.

We are here to commemorate the massacre at Deir Yassin, on 9 April 1948. It was the first out of an estimated five hundred villages on an ongoing plan of destruction of Palestinian life, which is still going on to this day.

Deir Yassin. It sounds like the start of an endearment.

It was not the most horrific of the massacres, even though ninety-three to 170 people were killed: bodies abused, women raped and thirty babies murdered.

Deir Yassin represents the first step of Plan Dalet, the Zionist plan to take over Palestine and expel the indigenous population by force.

There is a poignancy, that here, on the other side of the world, in this cold Scottish city, is a monument to remember these victims of airbrushed history. A British film about Palestine, *The Present* wins the British Short Film award at the BAFTAs. The director, Farah Nabulsi, gives a moving speech: 'I dedicate this film to the people of Palestine for whom freedom and equality is long, long overdue.'

There have been few opportunities for Gerry and me, as Palestinian activists, to protest against the Israeli occupation of Palestine in this Covid year. Our last act of protest was in October for the Israel-Scotland football match. I took a fantastic photo of a police van with our poster superimposed in front of it: "Don't play ball with Israeli Apartheid".

Seven

Glinting in Spring

I'm not adding this year to my age. I didn't use it.

Anon

"You have all got wasps in your knickers" as my Aunt Teresa would have said, shaking an admonishing finger. Yes, these are our bees in our bonnets, our ants in our pants, our raison d'être. We are truly bothered. A whole year of lockdown has gone past: twelve long months. We are desperate to be allowed out of our cages, scratching at the bars, mouthing "help!". *Au Secours!*

The prospect of travelling to France for the Easter holidays has evaporated, even though Gerry, officially an NHS worker, has had his two *jags*. He is officially "Two *Jags* Gerry". He struts around, doing the shopping, out to work on a daily basis and bringing back news of the outside world to my purdah state.

Meanwhile, I have a skin biopsy and a mole is cut out of my back. I am told that I cannot do housework for some time. When I joyously relate this to Gerry, who now has this, on top of his cooking duties, to contend with, he looks none too pleased and demands written confirmation from the doctor. I show him the well-sewn stitches as proof. 'No bending,' I add, helpfully. The downside is that I cannot sleep on my back. There is truly a niche market missing in the NHS – "breastie nesties" – whereby a mattress has two holes cut out for perfect comfort. FOMO – fear of missing out – has passed us by. HOGO – hassle of going out – has come over us. We are not doing anything or going anywhere: *stasis in perfecto*. Gerry spends his time accumulating keyboards in his music room, headphones firmly clamped to his ears.

When my friend Lisa asks me to join her "virtual" book group, I am delighted to do so. My aversion to clubs has now dissipated. Besides, as Lisa explains, this *Bibliofilles* group is completely pretentious, as we choose books by foreign writers that have been translated into English. We are true armchair travellers. After all, armchair travelling is all we can do throughout this pandemic. So far, we have been introduced to the mindsets of Swedish, Norwegian, Syrian, American, Italian and, *bien sûr, les français*. I now completely understand the concept favoured by so many French writers, *le nombrilisme*. In other words, navel-gazing. To generalise wildly, it is their love of interior worlds, philosophy and intellectual sparring, with no sense of humour whatsoever, which makes French writers, especially those in Parisian *salons*, so distinctive.

I have gone back to reading D.H. Lawrence, a favourite author of mine when I was a teenager. As an aging adult, what strikes me are all the references to the Driving Force and the penchant for CAPITALS. In the famous 1960 trial for obscenity regarding his novel *Lady Chatterley's Lover*, the jury was asked: 'Is it a book that you would even wish your wife or your servants to read?'

The pandemic has allowed us to take a peek at the intimate life of others. My pupils have a good idea of the *guddle* in which I live. Now that they tune into my live broadcasts, all the way from fragrant Ruchill, Rocco the dog has been introduced as an icebreaker into my teaching. He has even barked in reply to a pupil's dog. The backgrounds of TV presenters' homes are fascinating, usually consisting of bookshelves of specially chosen books, some colour coordinated. There is apparently a warehouse somewhere in England that sells books by the metre for background purposes in order to boast of your impressive display of knowledge. I note the placement of hip items – a Warholesque take of the Queen, a picture of the Daleks from the *Doctor Who* series – or "naughty" items such as nipple tassels to lend a slight frisson. The latest must-have for the more patriotic is an array of flags festooning living rooms or studies; some appear to be shooting out of the ears of the talking heads.

The swan couple now have four eggs in the nest and Prince Philip has died just short of his hundredth birthday. According to a friend who has just retired from her job in the BBC, it is a sackable offence if the instructions on broadcasting the death of a senior royal are not carried out to the letter. Full mourning descends on the BBC, which records 116,000 complaints. One curious fact: Prince Philip's parents met at Queen Victoria's funeral in 1901. As far as I am concerned, the prince is redeemed by being a recipient of Denmark's Order of the Elephant. Also, by designing a classy, customised hearse Land Rover for his own mortal remains.

'Gerry, my man-liege,' I command, 'pick up your hammer; put on your bonnet; and get to work on my chariot.'

'No problem, ma'am,' mutters Gerry, 'you'll be on the other side of the Styx in a jiffy.'

Another fact of wonderment and completely random is that Lenin spoke perfect English with a Dublin accent. His old English teacher had come from Ireland. Why have these gems been hidden away for so long?

'What's with the elephant face?' asks Eunice tactlessly. It's true; my face has blown up and my eyes are slits; my breathing is laboured. I have been waiting almost a year to be seen by the allergies clinic, but of course non-emergencies have been put on the back burner. It's the same waiting game for the MRI scan on my clicky knee, which I call my housemaid's knee. The genuflexion years are truly over.

'Honestly, I'm quite alright,' I answer weakly, at which protestation I am bundled into the car by Gerry and driven down to the doctor's surgery and plied with a glorious cocktail of painkillers etc. Eventually, the swelling subsides.

It doesn't help that I am so unfit. Apparently, I have put on nine Covid kilos since this time last year. When I walk up the stairs – *click, click, click* – my bottom follows obediently a few nanoseconds behind me.

On 16 April 2021, restrictions are lifted slightly, and we are allowed out of our Glasgow cage. It is an auspicious day, the Feast Day of Saint Drogo of Sebourg. I wonder if it was chosen on purpose. Reportedly, Drogo was able to bilocate, to maintain his actual presence in two totally different places at the same time. This is obviously what we need in times of catch-up. So much to do, places to see, people to meet. Drogo is patron saint of shepherds, coffee and the ugly, which is quite a varied calling.

I slap on muscle rub and wrap a bandage around my knee and, together with Rocco and Gerry, walk slowly up and down the Kilpatrick Hills. Saint Rocco is the patron saint of pandemics, so having him in canine form beside us augurs well. The sun is out and the air sparkles like champagne; the walk is not too arduous. I have walking poles to help me.

Looking over the valley to the other side of the Clyde, the warm sun is on our faces. The last lines of Edwin Muir's poem, "Strawberries" spring to mind:

> let the sun beat
> on our forgetfulness
> one hour of all
> the heat intense
> and summer lightning
> on the Kilpatrick hills
>
> let the storm wash the plates

The flourish of that last line; that perfect moment of happiness, tossed to the winds.

The date of release coincides with going back to work in school, *bien sûr*! Nevertheless, there is a spin of activity: visiting my mother and her partner, Douglas, in Ayr – *oh the sea at last*. Then a magnificent drive to Tighnabruaich to meet up with Bridget and Keith in their spanking-new, funky café. Followed by a walk in deserted Otter Ferry, the languorous meal outside with Susan and Ian in Bridge of Weir. *It was too hot outside but who cares*. We were cooled by a 99 ice cream on Troon Beach with Christine. We loved sitting in Ann's garden in Lochwinnoch speaking of nothing in particular. My cup overfloweth! We have hardly seen anyone for six months!

Everyone has a lockdown tale to tell. To mitigate her loneliness, Christine volunteered to clean the local church, singing as she deployed her duster. One day, the head cleaner turned up and spoke to her sternly: 'Just to say, Christine, that our Lord can tell if you have dusted underneath the pews.'

The mad dash of it all, seeing all these well-loved faces once more. The crowning glory, a visit to the hairdressers.

Harris & Lewis 2021 *Shimmering*

The sight of the big man's white bottom hovering like a blancmange in the window opposite me was not the sea view I had been promised.

It all began with Gerry asking, 'Where would you like to go for your special birthday?' My birthday is a week before Christmas, so it is usually buried underneath the tinsel. 'Shall I book somewhere in the October week holiday?' He knew that for years I have been hankering to go to Scarista House in the Outer Hebrides and stride out on the Luskentyre Sands in Harris.

The Outer Hebrides at last!

Step we gaily, on we go, heel for heel and toe for toe

I pack warm clothes and my walking boots.

Arm in arm, and row and row

Can't wait to go.

All for Mairi's wedding

The happiest song to hum.

Sharon had just died in October 2020 and her funeral was arranged for that week with Covid lockdown.

'I think we should still go away to Ullapool, just for one night, for a change of scene,' suggested Gerry. He brightened up. 'We still have the booking for the inn with the sea view. At least we can watch the ferry departing for Stornoway.' I nodded dumbly. We decided to drive up to Inverness the night before, so at least we would have a full day in Ullapool.

It had been almost impossible to find anything suitable in the Covid window, so we settled on a cut-price twin bedroom in an industrial park in Inverness. The next day, we were directed to a suitable coastal walk for people with a dog around Scourie. This is an abandoned village on the headland, along a stunning narrow road with New Age dwellings dotted around. The sea meandered tantalisingly below. However, Rocco would have to navigate the steep cliffs to get there. He pulled at his lead in frustration. It was a Virginia Woolf moment. Nothing was quite as it should be. Hadn't Virginia Woolf visited the Western Isles and written about it? I ask Gerry. *To the Waves, at the Lighthouse*, something like that? Maybe *From the Waves, up the Lighthouse*? 'Oh aye, I think it was called *Virginia Woolf and the Hebrides*,' said Gerry, knowledgeably.

'*Virginia Woolf and the Crying Weans*?' I teased. 'Or was it not,' I said, looking at Rocco, '*Virginia Woolf and the Mastiff Hounds*?' Whatever, it was not a comedy.

The promised sea view was not funny either. If the hotel in

front were to be demolished, then, granted, the sea would be seen. Until then, our window looked directly into the window in front. Could it be worse? Suddenly, blancmange man turned round. It can always be worse! Sometimes, the funny side is the only side to look at. We watched the Stornoway ferry depart in the morning without us. We turned on our tyres and drove back to Glasgow.

There have been other signs that Lewis and Harris have sent off warning signals to evade us. At a visit to the British Museum in London, specifically to ogle the finery of the Anglo-Saxon Sutton Hoo helmet, we were furious to discover, on leaving the museum, that right across from the mask were the twelfth-century ivory Lewis chessmen. All but eleven pieces are found today in the British Museum. We had been so intent admiring the elaborately crafted helmet, that we had not even noticed them. This omission necessitated a return visit to the museum specifically for the chessmen. This precious exhibit is for the Scots what the Elgin Marbles are to the Greeks. Send them homewards!

It wasn't till the summer of 2021 that the window of opportunity to visit the Hebrides presented itself once more. By that time, Glasgow had been in lockdown for nearly nine months. A gestation longer than any other region in Scotland. Locked down in Tier Three, whilst the rest of the country is out gambolling. As the man from the wireless intoned cheekily, 'Glasgow is like the slow child in the back of the class.'

As soon as we could, at the start of summer 2021, we skedaddled up north, taking our Covid lateral flow tests before, during and after our escape. Our "gagging kit", as I call it. The west coast glistened in the early evening sun, preening and posturing, as one spectacular vista gave way to the next. Up through to the tip of Skye and the short crossing over from Uig to Tarbert on Harris. Our plans were nearly scuttled, yet again, when the ferry we had booked on for the return journey from Stornoway to Lewis broke down and the repairs looked set to be many weeks rather than a couple of days. 'If need be, I'll put on my floats and swim over the Minch,' I told Gerry grimly.

'I can't believe we are here!' I said, breathlessly, taking in the all-encompassing view of the swirling sands of Luskentyre, the iridescent light forming patterns on the shore. 'Best of all, we are the only ones here. Where is the rest of the world?' Locked-in, I expect. By the time we reached Scarista House, we were in a bubble of joy. More bubbles then appeared. Our lovely friends, Ron and Julie in Newfoundland, had ordered a bottle of champagne to await us to celebrate our arrival. In the event, it had been waiting there since October! Newfoundland is directly across this huge expanse of water. If only we could spirit them over the Atlantic towards us. The owners of Scarista House, Tim and Patricia Martin, upgraded us to a suite with a deck behind the main house. This met with Rocco's approval. He sprawled along the deck, eyeing up the beach below, calling to him like a siren. We watched the orange sun go down over the Harris hills, feeling exhausted but blissfully happy.

The next day was a Labrador's delight: six empty white beaches and no human in sight. At dinner the previous evening, we met a local man and his daughter. They were an encyclopaedia of Hebridean knowledge. 'Why do they say that Harris and Lewis are two islands when they are in fact one island?' I asked.

'Well,' the wise man answered, 'once you go past the Harris hills and the flat lands appear, then that is the border. They speak a different Gaelic from us, in the north.'

'What do you think of all the new houses that have been built in recent years?' I had been admiring the glass, steel and wooden structures completely in tune with the landscape. I especially admired the hobbit-like houses that seemed to peep out of the hillsides. Stuart Bagshaw is the architect who spearheaded the style coined "Hebrinavean", a mix of the local with a sleek Scandinavian feel.

'That's all well and good,' he replied, 'but locals can't afford to buy them. What cost £80k last year now costs £250k. And you have to be wealthy to be able to rent around here. All these incomers now...' His voice trailed off. 'But, on the other hand,' he perked up, 'if they are young incomers with young children and skills, then they are more than welcome.' In fact, since the creation of the local "Community Trusts", where locals made their own decisions, the outlook is fair in the islands. This was far from being the case for a long time.

'Where do you suggest we go tomorrow?' we asked our guide.

'You shouldn't miss "The Golden Road" – it tells you all the history of this place,' came his cryptic reply. This name is given, ironically, to the C79 road skirting lochans, twisting and turning over a lunar landscape. (Indeed, so out of this world it is that it was used to depict Jupiter in Stanley Kubrick's iconic film, *2001: A Space Odyssey.*) It was anticipated that the cost of blasting through such unforgiving rock to create the road would be prohibitive (hence ironically referring to it as golden), but such was the desire for the road to be built that many a local gave of their labour freely. In the end, the final cost was far lower than anticipated. What was surprising was the number of houses and hamlets, in a place where the soil is poor and unyielding. This was the result of the heinous crime of the highland clearances, when local people were turfed out of their homesteads by the landlords. Their houses were then demolished, to make way for deer or sheep. Most of the dispossessed people found a new life in Canada or made their way to the stony, less fertile "bays" of the east.

This strikes a personal chord. The clearances cast a shadow to this day. My Auntie Margaret and her sisters grew up in Kincraigie village near Dunkeld in Perthshire. Their father worked for the local landlord, as did all the other relatives in the village, as did their forefathers. The landlord refused to sell the tied cottages of the estate. However, my Auntie Margaret and my grandfather managed to rent a cottage there, where all the family visited throughout the years. I remember Old Aunt Maggie, who loved animals more than people, lived in the last cottage. She never married after she sued a would-be suitor for breach of promise for jilting her at the altar. Mr McLaren was the old shepherd who constantly walked up and down the village street and once asked me if the saddler's shop still existed in Argyle Street. He had last visited the big city in 1922. Auntie Margaret's father lived in a cottage in Kincraigie, as did Auntie Grace who had been born in Montana. Her parents had emigrated to the USA but had missed their native village so much that they returned after Grace's birth. Branches of the same family had lived in Kincraigie for generations, so it came as a complete shock when the laird of the estate decided there would be more profit in investing in shooting and using the cottages as accommodation for the wealthy gun-toting grouse shooters. This was in the 1980s. However, the evictions of more than a hundred years earlier had cast a long shadow. The inhabitants were given a few weeks to leave and unceremoniously turfed out. Occasionally, we make pilgrimages to the scene of happy childhood days. The one relative who did wander far is my Auntie Janet, who married Abed and moved to Beirut. My cousins were brought up in the Middle East, rather than the middle of Perthshire.

Five years ago, Gerry and I joined the Lebanese branch for a small family reunion in the village. The shooting venture had failed, and the cottages had either been sold off later for a healthy sum or let out for holidays. We posed for the family shot with big smiles which quickly turned to looks of horror as a military jet flew by, unnervingly low. For a moment, my cousins thought that the Israelis had come back to give them a good bombing. One they wouldn't forget! They all dived for cover.

Last year, Gerry and I joined my cousin Zeina and family for our usual get-together and walk up to the lochan in the hills. We parked the car in the spot which was beside a public right of way. Only to find on our return that someone had stuck a note in shouty letters that this was "PRIVATE LAND" and this was "HIS" parking spot. Nothing gets my hackles up more than this. I had to be restrained from knocking on his door and giving him a piece of my feverish mind or a well-placed wedgie. A similar thing had happened in France where people had decided to extend their privacy by denying others their right of freedom to roam. 'Why don't you pen a reply,' I ask Zeina, 'along the lines of "THIS IS OUR ANCESTRAL HOME WHICH WE ARE CLAIMING BACK. SO GET OOT!"'

It is therefore with pleasure that I view the success of the Land Reform Act introduced by the Scottish Government in 2003. More than half of the islands' area of the Outer Hebrides is now registered in "Community Trusts". These give crofters and communities the right to buy their own land and manage their own affairs. For the first time ever, islanders are in control of their own destiny.

Apart from the innovative architecture, the islands have rediscovered their natural larder and new food venues have popped up. Some with honesty boxes outside the door. Scarista House is known for its yummy fare and takes pride in not selling bottled water. As they put it, "when you have the purest water in the world coming out of your taps, why on earth would you import it?".

Refreshingly, the islands are still relatively free of crystals and angels' enterprises; the natives are too rooted in reality to fly away on fanciful ephemera. The church car parks are still packed on Sunday morning; the no-frills protestant hold still retains its grip. My curiosity is piqued (I am the inveterate nosey parker) by the church name in the village of Northton, "The Free Continuing Church". I had heard about the "Wee Frees", the breakaway group from the Church of Scotland in the mid-nineteenth century. The worshippers demanded that there be no state interference in the running of their church. The "Disruption" it was called, or the "rebellion of the pious". There is another wing called "The Wee Wee Frees", which houses the even more conservative Free Presbyterian Church of Scotland. Famously, the rule of the Sabbath is sacrosanct. No playing in playgrounds (the swings were chained together, lest you fell into temptation), no entertainment, no washing out to dry, no singing, no dancing, nothing open. After all, as my Auntie Margaret observed in jest, sex standing up might lead to dancing. The only thing open should be the Bible and the Lord's words imbibed. It is a hard God who would understand the life on such unforgiving shores. This extreme conservatism was still not fundamentalist enough. After a few scandals, a schism of the schism was formed in 2000. It can't be much fun for the visiting islanders of South Uist and Barra where Catholicism holds sway, especially when signs of "the Lord will smite Papists" (I paraphrase) can be found. Surely the best advert for the church, admittedly in Ullapool, is: "A church for everyone. No one is too bad to come in. No one is too good to stay away".

However, the Lord's Day Observance Society has observed some unwelcome cracks: Sunday flights to the mainland, a petrol station opening, ferry sailings. Here, in Northton, The Temple Café, a nod to a hobbit house in the distinctive Hebridean design, also opens on a Sunday, selling machair buns and strong coffee. We walk to the "temple", a ruined church, in the headland. Birds are nesting and squawking loudly. I stick my gloves into my hat in case of any skydiving attacks; apparently this has happened in the past. Farmers are cutting wads of peat with strange-shaped tools in long trenches.

Gerry tells me that ministers opposed the building of lighthouses in the mid-nineteenth century, because this would deny them "the spoils of the sea" in the event of shipwrecks. These provided the locals with much-needed sustenance from grinding poverty.

The constant sound of the cuckoo is reassuring. As we turn back towards Northton, we can see the shimmering membrane of shining sand in the distance. We amuse ourselves by making up silly tongue twisters.

'Miss, I was pished at Christmas in the isthmus.'

'Puffins puff whilst peregrines percolate.'

'Ye Canna eat yer Rhum'n'Eigg in Muck.'

When are tongue twisters ever serious?

Black-faced lambs stick close to their mothers. I teach Gerry a Polish childhood song: *Gdzie żeś ty bywał, czarny baranie* – Where have you been, black sheep? – and we both join in the baaing of the sheep at the end.

Gerry counters with his favourite mondegreens, the skewered lyrics of famous songs, a perfect example of cognitive dissonance, whereby the mind tries to make sense of the world.

You fill up my census. (You fill all my senses.) *I am the Lord of the damp settee.* (I am the Lord of the Dance, said he.) *The girl with colitis goes by.* (The girl with kaleidoscope eyes.) I weigh in with classical musical lines: *Salmon chanting evening.* (Some enchanted evening.) *Somewhere over the rainbow, weigh a pie.* (Somewhere over the rainbow, way up high.)

Gerry's late mother swore that she heard the lyrics, *I've got a sewing machine*, and not Hawkwind's "I've got a Silver Machine". At any rate, it made her happy.

The weather here in the Outer Hebrides is usually described in terms of misty, murky, mild and moist. Nevertheless, for the short time we are here in these islands, there seems to be celestial intervention.

'Just as well we brought sunscreen and shorts,' I say to the sunburnt Gerry, as we walk across the empty expanse of Luskentyre Beach. We look over the turtle outline of the tantalisingly beautiful, but uninhabited, island of Taransay. On one side of the island is the chapel of St Keith, where the men are buried, and on the other side is the women's burial ground of St Taran's. The reason that the population dwindled was a direct result of the massive rent hike in the mid-nineteenth century. Today, only fourteen out of 119 of the islands in the Outer Hebrides are populated.

We drive past the brooding Harris hills, past the sign of "Isle of Lewis" on the road. 'Looks like someone has just drawn an arbitrary line across from east to west; the Hebridean Sykes-Picot line,' remarks Gerry. We reach the Callanish Stones that dominate the flat landscape. The stone circle and the avenue are older than Stonehenge, older than the pyramids of Giza. There is something almost human in the shape of the stones with faces carved at the top. The only other visitors today are three girls from Paraguay in shorts. I try to hug the stones, a borrower against an amazon. I cut my palm on the sharp contours of the stone, and blood drips like stigmata. Lewis rock is the arthritic Labrador compared to the playful puppy rock of Iceland. Lewisian "gneiss", as it is called, is over three hundred million years old, battered by the elements, the oldest rock in the world. The boulders are called "erratics", deposited by the receding glaciers. They look as if they were dumped from a great height to land anywhere in any state. Careless boulders.

It is so peaceful and pleasant as we stroll over to Callanish 11 and Callanish 111, the smaller, friendlier brother and sister stone sites. The rock is just as proud and unforgiving. A memory slips into my mind. When the children were small, we joined my elder sister and family on holiday and found ourselves on a trip to the famous Staffa Island in the Inner Hebrides. As all the other adults explored Fingal's Cave, I was tasked to look after the four children on top of the island's volcanic terrain. Suddenly, the children broke free, and each child ran to their own compass point on the edge of the island, which gave way to sheer, basalt cliffs. I don't know how I did it, but I summoned up superhuman energy and ran like a dervish, rounding up each child before he/she plunged into the swirling sea below. By the time the adults re-emerged, I was a quivering wreck with four children hanging onto me. I still have nightmares to this day. Respect to sheepdogs.

The Callanishes of lesser importance seem untouched by the long hand of tourism, at least today. Sheep wander around and fleece winds itself around the stones. Rocco relishes the crusts of sheep poo. Gerry lies on the grass, taking photos of the monoliths, whilst Rocco licks his face with farty breath.

Step we gaily, on we go

To the broch at Carloway and the blackhouses at Gearrannan, with their low, thick walls and thatched roofs. It was only in the 1950s that electricity (and running water) was introduced to these original homes. I wonder if I am looking at the same houses my father connected to the National Grid. The contrast between his native Poland torn asunder by war, and these remote islands flung far out in the Atlantic must have been so striking. About sixty years ago, my father (who has now been dead for over forty years) had had a summer job erecting telegraph poles for electricity supply around the islands. Children usually don't find their parents remotely interesting, and it's only now, as a fully-fledged adult, that I long to ask him about his experiences.

Heel for heel and toe for toe

We travel through the bleak, flat landscape to Ness, the most north-westerly point in Europe. Gerry's friend, John Macleod, comes from here. John is now an architect and lives in Glasgow. He describes the pebble-dashed brown houses as "mean". So, I think he would be the first to celebrate the Hebridean renaissance. John is also the owner of Crabshakk, a hip seafood restaurant in Finnieston, in the West End of Glasgow, having fulfilled a lifelong dream of bringing to the table the freshest of seafood from the islands.

John used to tell Gerry tales of joining the "guga hunt" as a young lad. It is like a rite of passage for young men in Ness, in which they travel to the remote island of Sula Sgeir with the elders and live in stone bothies, originally monk dwellings. There, on the island, they spend a fortnight killing, skinning and smoking about two thousand young gannets (gugas) which they later bring home for the delectation of others. All the gugas would be fully accounted for!

John also speaks proudly of his namesake, his great-uncle John Finlay Macleod, a local hero. On 1 January 1919, a troop ship was bringing back 280 weary young men from World War One. They were all desperate to see their families and homes after the long years fighting in the trenches in France. Just yards from the shore, the ship hit the rocks known as the "Beasts of Holm", with Stornoway harbour a mile away. A total of 201, out of 280, men drowned. John's great-uncle managed to save seventy-nine of the local lads by swimming out from the ship with a line and then creating a human chain with others. The tragedy, the "Iolaire Disaster", has seared itself in the consciousness of such a tight society, which lost so much of its youth in one fell swoop.

Incidentally, the surname Macleod pops up again and again, giving rise to a sing-song – *Hey Macleod, Get Aff Of Ma Ewe* – a song about nature and its urges, by the band the Stony Rollers.

Lying on the deserted beach of Ness, the sun burning down on us, Rocco happily splashing his ball in a pool between rocks, seals somersaulting in the distance, Gerry sighs. 'Perfection in Ness, who would have thought?'

Arm and arm and row and row

Disappointingly, the Lews Castle Museum and Archive in Stornoway was closed due to Covid. It opened in 2016 and is a twenty-first-century state-of-the-art institution with interactive displays, telling of the past and present history of the islands. There is a fascinating story about Gerhard Zucker, a German rocket scientist who tried and tried again to send letters attached to a rudimentary rocket from the island of Scarp to Harris. He failed time and time again. It says much to the power of optimism. Or, as Homer Simpson might have put it: "Trying is the first step towards failure". Now, a drone would do the trick.

Scarp had already achieved fame of sorts as the home of Christina Maclennan, who became the only woman in the world to give birth to healthy twins on different islands in different weeks. I'll explain. Although Mrs Maclennan had given birth to a healthy child on 14 January 1934, she was still in great pain a day later. The pain was so intense it was decided that she would make the perilous journey in the middle of winter to Harris strapped on an open boat. When she had reached Harris, she was driven to the hospital in Stornoway on Lewis, where she gave birth to a healthy second twin. I cannot contemplate the suffering of this poor woman.

Stornoway looks attractive in the bright sunshine. My eye is drawn to the plaque on the corner of Keith Street: "FEMALE INDUSTRIAL SCHOOL 1848. A school to provide young ladies with the opportunities to learn a range of domestic activities and crafts". No doubt their skills would be put to good use in the burgeoning land of servants on the mainland. At least it is not as bad as my favourite gruesome description in Liverpool, "The Royal Hospital, previously named the Royal Institution for the Care, Training and Education of Idiots and Imbeciles".

A plaque is also on the outside wall of our hotel. It states that Prince Charles had ordered a cherry brandy at the Crowne Hotel in 1963 when he was only fourteen years old. The shame, the *stooshie*! His private detective was dismissed, and the scandal died down.

Flicking through the guidebook, I frown and turn to Gerry. 'Do you know what the elephant, actually elephants, in the room are round here? What is never discussed?' He isn't for guessing. 'Well, what's big, blonde and mouthy?' I ask.

'You?' answers Gerry and ducks.

'You *cheeky bizom!*' I reply. That boy takes liberties. 'Donald Trump *bien sûr!*'

Trump is proud of his Scottish heritage, which he cited to support his penchant for buying up Scottish golf courses. I recall a photo of him being taken outside the house where his mother had grown up. In fact, he stayed a total of ninety-seven seconds outside the house for the photo shoot.

Mary Anne MacLeod, his mother, is a fascinating figure. Her life encapsulates the Hebridean experience. Born in 1912, the youngest of ten children, she was brought up in a poor, Gaelic-speaking family in a croft in Tong, outside Stornoway. Her marriage prospects were limited: so many young men had died in World War One and then in the Iolaire Disaster. Her future seemed bleak: either working in the Harris Tweed or herring industries, or in service on the mainland of Scotland. Moreover, a scandal hung over the family in this deeply religious community. Her elder sister Catherine had given birth to a child out of wedlock. So, Mary did what countless poor Hebrideans had done before her; she emigrated to America in 1920 in search of a better life. It's clear that Donald had inherited his wild bouffant from his mother, but apart from that, she did not seem to have much influence on her son. On her deathbed in a New York hospital, she spoke only Gaelic, the language of her childhood. No one around her understood her final words. The Trump connection is not one the locals wish to discuss.

'So, what's the other elephant?' asks Gerry.

'Ah, yes, the bank fiasco!'

Comhairle nan Eilean Siar (The Council of the Western Isles) had invested – and lost – the whopping sum of £23 million in the three biggest banks in Iceland, brought down in the global financial crash of 2008. It is testimony to the resilience of the islanders that they have somehow weathered the storm of this disaster, just like all the other disasters that have befallen them in the past.

'Come on, wake up, Basia, you have to see this!' Gerry is shaking me from my slumbers.

I rub my eyes. 'What are you on about?' It is a pleasant crossing over to Ullapool and I had been snoozing below deck.

'It's a winky male, come on!' 'A what?' And there, following the boat, a pod of minke whales, a white flash skirting the waves, escorting us to our next destination.

All for Saffy's pakoras...

Saffy and Andrew are originally from the middle of England but spent a few years in Glasgow, where we met them. They had moved up to their dream home outside Ullapool in mid-winter, during a brief hiatus in the pandemic, knowing no one. Saffy ran a vegan café in Glasgow, and, true to form, the smell of freshly made pakoras lure us into the house. Our friends have since completely embraced Highland life and are equally embraced by the local population, as they are not retired. They have brought a much-needed addition of children to the local school. Even better, the whole family is learning to speak Gaelic. Looking for the ladies' toilet on the boat coming over, I inadvertently walked through the door marked *Fir*, deducing that it couldn't be the gents' toilets marked *Mnàthan*. I quickly realised my mistake and made a sharp exit.

The weather is still clement, and Saffy says casually, 'I wonder what the midges are like.' I look at her with disbelief.

'You wonder what the midges are like!' I squeak. 'This is the west coast where these buggers are lethal.' I nearly lie on my back and *shoogle* my legs around in astonishment. Midges are the devil's curse. 'Don't tell me you chose to live here, and you don't know what the midges are like?'

'Well, we once came here on holiday in September and the weather was fine…' Saffy's voice trails off weakly. 'Mind you, I did get bitten by something yesterday.'

'You'll be needing the full beekeeper's regalia,' I warn her.

Driving home in the semi-darkness of early summer, I think of the haunting, elegiac music of St Kilda. An old, reclusive man in a care home in Edinburgh played these tunes on the piano. His piano teacher had been one of the islanders who had been taken off the island in 1930, when life there became untenable.

Again, a portent, a sign, popping up to mock my cynicism. Flicking through the TV channels at home, we stumble across a documentary, *The Scottish Island that Won the Lottery*. It recounts how the islanders of North Uist won the People's Postcode Lottery; a little bit for everyone, which was life-transforming. Crofters generally earn £2k a year, so most islanders have a smattering of wee jobs to boost their income. After the win, one invested in a comfy chair, another a cattle grid, another a wheelbarrow. His old one was fifty years old, tied together with bits of wood. 'So, what will you do with the old one?' he was asked.

'I think I might try to sell it,' he replied. I understand completely where he is coming from. Our own wheelbarrow in Coutal is nicely bashed up, tips over easily and is held together with wood and ropes. It will last another few years, with a few more patchings.

We will return to the Western Isles one day; after all, I have a long-standing date with St Kilda.

There will be no wedding!

Nine

May & June 2021
Inside and Outside World

If you are neutral in situations of injustice,
you have chosen the side of the oppressor.
If an elephant has its foot on the tail of a
mouse and you say that you are neutral,
the mouse will not appreciate your neutrality.

Archbishop Desmond Tutu

The swans are hungry. Every morning when I wake up, I look out of the window and see one waiting patiently to be fed at our quayside, whilst the other is sitting on the eggs, long neck curled over her body, a feather pillow. It can't be long till the hatching. Visitors stop by constantly, to worship at the swan shrine, keeping a respectful distance.

On my daily swan-watch, I catch the pen rearranging the

eggs, nudging them around the nest. They must be ready to crack open; I wonder if she feels the movement of her chicks. The male is on guard, his feet firmly planted by the nest, protecting his family. The very next day, I spy three fluffy dark cygnets, peeking out from under their mother's body. Immediately, the mother whacks them with her long neck, back to safety beneath her undercarriage. She must be absolutely *scunnered*. Her chicks are curious, as if saying, '*Coucou* world, here we are!' Another two join their siblings to complete the family.

Nonchalant Rocco shows no interest at all in swans; he is far more interested by the feast of bread surrounding the nest, and he happily chomps away by my side.

I am also busy happily chomping and regretting that my backside again obediently follows me up the stairs. However, this is not the reason that I sign up for the ten thousand steps a day in May for MAP, Medical Aid for Palestine. So far, I have managed to step up to the challenge. I have found that having a dog certainly helps. Although, I have resorted at times to jogging on the spot at the end of the evening, just to ensure I have achieved my goal.

***

The new Alba political party comes in to join the other parties displaying electoral wares for our delectation. We fully expected a hoo-ha in the build-up to the Scottish general election. Instead, a strangely muted, Covid-covered election takes place on 6 May. The weather hasn't helped, as it is freezing. In fact, it is snowing in many places in the north. As they say, *Na'er cast a cloot till May is oot.* In other words, don't lower your weather guard in Scotland, where a beautifully warm day can be followed by an icy blast. (I only found out recently that the "May" flower in this proverb is the May flower of the hawthorn tree. You can take off your winter attire when the May blossom is on the hawthorn tree.) Layers are the answer. Keep a cardie handy at all times. Maybe that should be a Public Health announcement!

As predicted, the SNP (Scottish National Party) are returned back in power in Scotland. The English electioneering machine was in full throttle the night before voting began in England. It was announced that the post-Covid economic recovery was predicted to be better than that after World War Two. A possible blockade by fishermen in Jersey led to France threatening to turn off the lights on the island. The jingoism was underlined by a period-costumed English soldier sounding off his musket. Ah, the theatricality of it all. However, it is a ruse that clearly worked, as even diehard towns such as Hartlepool voted Conservative.

I take comfort from Irvine Welsh's views on Scottish independence. He dismissed the notion it would lead to "conflict, hatred and distrust" between England and Scotland as the mindset of "opportunistic status quo fearmongers" and "gloomy nationalist fantasists".

> *Swedes, Norwegians and Danes remain on amicable terms; they trade, cooperate and visit each other socially any time they like",* he wrote. *"They don't need a pompous blustering state called Scandinavia, informing them from Stockholm how wonderful they all are but (kind of) only meaning Sweden.*
>
> Irvine Welsh, 16 May 2021, *The National.*

It's clear that the Tories care *hee-haw* about Scotland. Boris Johnson wins comfortably in England despite all the mounting evidence of his naughty ways. Once more, his nimble fashion of untangling himself from many a legal loophole triumphs.

The only thing I find truly fascinating about Johnson is that his great-grandmother, Helen Tracy Lowe-Porter, was the official translator of nearly all of Thomas Mann's works from German to English.

David Cameron, like many others, has been caught with his hand in the sweetie jar. I cannot help but recall his old catchphrase of "hugahoodie" and how it has such resonance today. "Carrie Antoinette", as Boris Johnson's wife has been dubbed by the press, is lambasted for redecorating way past the annual £30k limit allowed for the Downing Street flat. It is said to be in a tasteful Rococo style reminiscent of Tunnock's teacakes. Apparently, Dominic Cummings knows where the bodies are buried, but he isn't telling anyone… yet.

The school where I work is also used as an electoral polling station. So, all day we hear the hollering of all the candidates outside. One Nicola Sturgeon, whose ward this is in the south side of Glasgow, is busy schmoozing with the public outside the building. I could throw a pail of water out the window to quieten the din…

A week later, the DUP (Democratic Unionist Party) win again in Northern Ireland. A new leader is at the helm with the Dickensian name of Edwin Poots. He is a flat earth and creationist believer. He lasts two seconds, before he is cast aside. Mark Drakeford of the Labour Party wins again in Wales. There could not be a more Disunited Kingdom.

Back in February, we listened to a radio programme, *Ten lessons about the vaccination that Israel can teach the world*, as it is the first country that has vaccinated nearly all its citizens. No one understands why other small countries with greater wealth are not first in line in buying the vaccines. Someone phones up to ask why the 4.6 million Palestinians living in the occupied West Bank and the Gaza Strip (with the exception of those living in East Jerusalem) are not vaccinated, and the radio host briskly cuts them off, saying, 'This is not about politics.' A few days later, an Israeli politician explains that it is because Israelis pay their taxes. No one mentions the longest occupation in recent memory. The Israeli health minister, Edelstein, revealed that Israel was "seriously discussing" providing them with vaccinations. The vaccine "divide" exposes the cruel nature of occupation. Where is the international outrage directed at occupation, dispossession and collective punishment?

Two months after our last meeting, Naomi (from Scottish Jews Against Zionism) and I have organised another informal gathering as a mark of solidarity and reflection around the Deir Yassin memorial in a Glasgow park. It is Nakba Day, 15 May. We both give speeches with different perspectives. The Nakba, the Palestinian Catastrophe, is marked every year and refers to the ethnic cleansing of Palestine and near total destruction of Palestinian society in 1948.

Two events have triggered a full-blown war: Israeli troops have stormed the Al-Aqsa Mosque in Jerusalem during Ramadan and assaulted worshippers there, and Israeli settlers have expelled Palestinians out of their homes in Sheikh Jarrah in East Jerusalem. In retaliation, rockets have been fired from Gaza to Israel in support of their fellow Palestinians.

The images and film footage of spontaneous protests by millions of people all over the world marching for human rights for Palestinians keeps the glimmer of hope alive that there is still compassion in people's hearts. It is in President Netanyahu's interests that the focus is deflected from his pending trial for corruption. It suits his purposes that a war-like situation exists so that he is deemed "indispensable". As the head of government, his position lends him immunity from prosecution.

Nevertheless, it seems to be a strategy that has backfired.

Even the state-backed media cannot stem the flood of complaints about the bias of its reportage. The official line is: "Israel is unwillingly fighting a war of self-defence in Gaza, after hostilities were commenced by an aggressive Hamas military attack". Even the most politically unaware have noticed the bombastic language used by the BBC, with scenes of carnage in the background: "bombardments in Israel and in Gaza have killed 250 people". Usually, Palestinians (especially children) die, whilst Israelis are killed. The language goes on: "Israel has a right to defend itself", "clashes", "skirmishes", "tensions", "conflict"... Many reports are prefaced, "Iranian-backed Hamas terrorists". I think people have just had enough and, miraculously, have started to dig the truth out. One of the most moving speeches I have heard for a long time is by Baroness Warsi, speaking passionately about the hypocrisy in the way the Palestinians are portrayed.

Three spontaneous, defining protests have occurred in Glasgow in the last two weeks. Two of them I find life-affirming, make me proud to be Glaswegian. The other, a fifteen thousand-strong show of football hooliganism.

The first happened in Kenmure Street in the south side of Glasgow in one of the most multicultural areas of the city. Coincidentally, it is a part of Nicola Sturgeon's constituency. It happened when a man discovered that his two neighbours were about to be deported in a UK government Home Office dawn raid. He alerted his friends and soon a small crowd swelled to a few hundred. Another neighbour chained himself under the police van. Such an action by the authorities was especially inflammatory, as it took place during Eid al-Fitr, the Muslim festival that marks the end of Ramadan. The support of the local crowd won out and the Glasgow police accepted that the community was pursuing a greater good. This is civil disobedience at its best. One of the protesters, Pinar Aksu, commented, in an echo of the defiant words of John Smeaton, the aforementioned Glasgow baggage handler who foiled the terrorist attack at Glasgow Airport: 'They messed with the wrong city. This is just the start. When there is another dawn raid in Glasgow, the same thing will happen.'

The next event brought together fifteen thousand people, mostly young, to protest at the bombing of Gaza. Despite the serious message, there was a carnival atmosphere that prevailed in the bright sunshine. We marched towards BBC headquarters, chanting, 'Shame on you,' making a clear point about the media disinformation broadcast thus far.

The next day, we heard the BBC reportage, which, true to form, described, "Two marches took place in the city, one of Rangers fans and the other to support the situation in Israel and Palestine".

'Shame on you, BBC,' shouts Gerry at the screen and clambers onto our roof to stick up the Palestinian flag before banging out some tunes on his piano.

A similar number of Rangers football fans marched to George Square after winning the cup for the first time in ten years. The march descended into drunken violence and vandalism, leaving glass and rubbish strewn on the city streets. The clean-up bill was £60k. Not Glasgow's proudest moment.

What a difference a year can make. Now to be out on the streets, to meet friends at last. The previous May was complete lockdown. Once, I was stopped by police whilst walking the dog and told, in no uncertain terms, that it was luck that I was out walking the dog. Otherwise, "questions would have to be asked". No one could travel; people died alone; numbers were restricted at funerals. The weight of loss was heavy in the air.

***

Working as a teacher is turgid. We are now back in class. For authorities, to think that pupils would obediently stick to the two-metre rule is laughable; they are teenagers, for God's sake! Little can be done in the way of sanctions for bad behaviour, sorry, challenging behaviour. Everyone has to wear masks at all times, which in a strange way, seems to affect my hearing. Not good if you are a language teacher. No doubt many insults are muttered behind a mask by both teachers and pupils: dick, wanker and other choice words too lewd to repeat. I speak for myself.

Gerry suggests I get a sponsor for my visor. I don't understand. He adds helpfully, 'You know, you can offer your services as an ad-visor!'

After being told that the exams would be cancelled for another year, the SQA, Scottish Qualifications Authority, announces an about-turn. The exams will in fact take place after all. However, these exams will not be called exams in this instance, and teachers will have to moderate. It is an attempt to avoid a repeat of last year's exam fiasco, whereby initially 124,565 exam grades were lowered based on an algorithm. This marked down pupils who lived in poorer postcodes. Only when the (highly) articulate pupils took to the streets to protest against this potentially life-changing discrimination, was the unfairness rectified. A few years earlier, at the height of Corbyn-bashing, the media accused him of "broadband communism" after he said that every child should have access to the internet. Now internet inequality is apparent, as homeschooling has been a way of life for most pupils.

I teach at the epicentre of Covid city, Glasgow South, and the absence rate soars through the roof. It's a petri dish of contagion.

As soon as we spy a senior pupil, we grab them and make them sit an exam, sorry, test, for the Alternative Certification Model. This means that the pupils are sitting the same tests/ exams on different days. It is discovered, surprise, that some answers have been posted on TikTok and other internet sites. Evidently, there is a certain amount of cheating going on. It is an impossible situation. Given that so many marks are given to the speaking element in languages, this is less of a problem for our modern languages department than for others.

***

It's been such a long time since we have been outside our Glasgow prison compound, but as soon as we can, we head out with friends recently arrived from London to picnic beside Rob Roy's Grave in the Trossachs. Freedom!

Another day, Fran and I have a grand day out to the big smoke: Edinburgh. The city is just an hour away from Glasgow by train. Until recently, people were fined for travelling this short distance without an ironclad excuse. Our tourist destination is Mary King's Close, situated in the underbelly of the city where tightly packed medieval buildings huddled together just off the High Street. The ubiquitous Mary, Queen of Scots (and France) found herself held prisoner in the *close*; then, soon after, she was shunted hither and thither before her head was chopped off. At the time of Mary's incarceration, Scotland was going through a mini Ice Age and the landscape was bleak and almost treeless. In all, life appeared pretty miserable.

Buildings at that time were tall and narrow; the wealthiest lived in the top floors and the poorest at the bottom. Some twenty people were packed in each small, airless room with a toilet bucket (no fancy chamber pot), the contents of which would be tossed into the alleyway with a quick warning "Gardyloo!" (from the French *garde à l'eau*). The effluent then flowed into the pond at the bottom of the hill, where bodies and clothes were infrequently washed. In the seventeenth century, unsurprisingly, bubonic plague broke out in this midden, and disease would regularly spread like the pimples on a teenager's face. Eventually, at the turn of the twentieth century, these buildings were lopped and fell into disuse, emerging as a tourist attraction one hundred years later. We stepped out from the gloom, culturally sated. 'Shopping and drinkies, Fran?' The only way is up.

***

It's just as well we have the Eurovision Song Contest on the TV for some light relief. Although, sadly, much of the kitsch, schmaltzy and downright awful contestants have been pushed out by earlier elimination. We introduced our Austrian friend, Margritta, to our obsession with Eurovision some years back. Since then, we have kept up a running joke about a mournful song featuring "apricot stones", during which a man swung stones around his head. Margritta has occasionally sent an envelope with stones in it, no message but message received loud and clear. Since then, we have discovered apricot stones contain cyanide, so maybe she was sending a veiled message. We mourn the absence of Russian grandmothers baking bread and one iconic Polish entry with a young maiden in a low-cut top swinging her breasts as she churned butter while singing about "giving you all my Slavic loving". Apparently, Greta Thunberg's mother was once a Eurovision contender. This year, they have a fair share of scantily clad nubile females shaking their booties. Obviously, it's the quality of the songs that count. However, there is enough wackiness to satiate us.

The Icelanders in sweaters look like a 1960's folk band, and the French chanteuse giving a full-throated Piaf belter sounds like red wine, louche bars, smoke and heartbreak. I urge anyone who needs convincing of the entertainment value to watch Will Ferrell's film *Eurovision Song Contest: The Story of Fire Saga*, about the contest. Fiction that borders on the truth.

***

The G7 Summit in June 2021 on climate change takes place in Cornwall. The motto is: "Building Back Better". Boris Johnson takes a flight from London to Truro. I take this in with disbelief. He really does fly from London to Cornwall. Climate change gets short shrift, as legal loopholes are discussed. Pious leaders state that they are nearer their Paris Summit pledges but not quite there because so many compromises have to be made. The advent of "sausage wars" hardly helps matters. The European Union does not consider British sausages to be of EU standard (I quite like the sawdust taste) and therefore they are banned from Northern Ireland. The fallout from Brexit trundles on and Johnson looks frozen out from the rest of the EU leaders in Cornwall. Clearly, he is no longer welcome at the club. When questions are asked about the Brexit agreement, Ursula von der Leyen, President of the European Commission, replies witheringly: 'The Brexit agreement was written in English so that you can understand it.'

Covid cases soar during the Summit. Apparently, the hundreds of security guards from all over the world, most of whom haven't been tested, have been sneaking from their main accommodation ship to sample the Cornish nightlife on shore. They make sure the local population is left with a present they will never forget.

Despite this, Britain is doing well in the Covid vaccination programme, although it is reported that many people do not take up the offer of the *jag*. Not surprisingly, given that five blue NHS envelopes have come through our door for people who no longer live at this address.

Happily, I am now "Two *Jags* Basia" on a par with "Two *Jags* Gerry". The man beside me at the vaccination centre complains that there is blood on his shirt and asks why he wasn't given a plaster. I suspect he is looking for compensation, but the nurse smiles sweetly and sends him on his way. Our certificates saying that we are double *jagged* arrive and now we only need the PCR test and *maybe* we can go to France. Uncertainty prevails; one moment tourists are flocking to Portugal and then Portugal is placed on the amber list and the flocking stops abruptly.

At last, my long-awaited NHS consultations come through. Both are by telephone. It's difficult to describe the woeful state of my knee, so I helpfully put the phone towards it. 'Do you hear that?' I ask. 'When I bend my knee, it clicks and grinds!' The physio laughs.

The consultation regarding my many allergies ends with, 'Ah, I see. I suggest we do tests to ascertain the cause.' Back to square one.

What really takes the biscuit is the announcement of the imminent closure after a hundred years of the McVitie's biscuit factory in the East End of Glasgow and services to the Glasgow diet. To rub butter into the mix, they are just relocating down the road to Carlisle. My cupboards are now bulging with digestives. *On est à la gorge* – we have reached our limits.

What next? The demise of the Empire biscuit and pineapple cake? My spare tyres are expanding, as my world is rapidly crumbling.

Ten

Aquitaine Summer 2021 *Goldlight*

There must be some way out of here...

'Could you just check in online?' I ask Gerry. School's out for summer and we are due to fly out to Bergerac the next morning. Not so fast. The flights have been cancelled. We chuck what we can into the car and get ready for the long haul south, through England and France. We have certificates for our two *jags* and the results of our negative PCR tests. The time window for escape is narrow. 'Let me not forget my adrenaline squirt,' I remind myself, as I look around for my EpiPen. We do not want a repeat dash to hospital.

'That's not a nice way to talk about me,' pipes up Gerry.

'What?' I query.

'Squirt I am not,' he replies sternly.

Had we had enough time, we would have swerved to

Edinburgh and picked up Sharon's ashes. Not taking Rocco has liberated the back seat so we can swap over the driving every two hours and stretch out in the back, only stopping for the two Ps: petrol and pee. 'Umm… I have an appointment at 3.45pm… not for long though…'

Gerry eyes me suspiciously. 'What are you up to?'

'Just having a manicure and a pedicure, this and that…' It's been a long time without maintenance, I justify myself.

'In that case,' replies Gerry, 'I'm taking my piano to France; no back seat loitering for you! That's where it will be parked!'

We whip through England and reach the Channel Tunnel in record time, only to be told that one form is missing. Gerry had been meticulous in following the Covid instructions. It turns out that it is the form that says you have brought all the other bits of necessary paper which is missing. There is a reason why bureaucracy is a French word. Even border control realised that maybe this was one form too many.

We are in France! That it is to say that the train has stopped in France. Nothing happens. Eventually, it is announced that the doors are malfunctioning. For a split second it looks like the train is on the way back to Blighty. There is a solution: we must all reverse down the train. The Italian driver behind us finds this an impossible manoeuvre and he and the car go off the rails. Just as he and his car stutter and splutter to the grand finale, it is announced that the doors are now functioning once more. We shoot out of the top like squeezed toothpaste, *encore en route*! At the same time, my stepfather, Douglas, texts from Kyle of Lochalsh, a small town in Scotland, across from the Isle of Skye. He is waiting at the train station. *There is actually a sign that says that if you want the train to stop you must put your hand out and make sure the driver sees you!* he informs us.

The sign for Sangatte – the erstwhile asylum seekers' jungle – pops up as we leave Calais. What happened to all these refugees, these people without homes? These people whom no one wanted. Did they just melt away or are they languishing in some temporary place?

Aquitaine, or to be precise, Nouvelle-Aquitaine, is the biggest administrative region in France. In 2016, three regions – Aquitaine, Limousin and Poitou-Charentes – were merged to form a land area of 84,000 square miles, bigger than Scotland! It seems somehow fitting that Scots are returning to revive the *Auld Alliance*, Scotland's most famous connection with France from the thirteenth century, with an agreement between the two countries to curtail English expansion. One of the greatest benefits of the *Auld Alliance* was that Scottish merchants were given the choice of the best of Bordeaux wines! At primary school, we had been taught that Scots did not need a passport to go over to France, if we could prove we were Scottish. Somehow, I think all these privileges lapsed some time ago.

'You know, Gerry,' I say hesitantly, 'I don't want to tempt fate, but maybe this is the first time in a very long time that we haven't had some French travel disaster…' I must have shaken fate out of its slumbers. As we near Aquitaine, I ask anxiously, 'Surely, we are not travelling towards the eye of this electric storm?' Which would be impressive if you were safe and warm in your home. However, not so when you are driving in a tin can with the rain hitting the windscreen so hard that the poor wipers just can't keep up and everything is a blur. Fine if you are half duck, but not if you are in a state past exhaustion. This is the *Rocky Horror Show* moment. Maybe we should stop at the gates of this crumbling château and seek refuge? Let the door be opened by a cadaverous creep and be swallowed up forever? Bring out the thunder! (God moving his furniture.) Bring out the lightning! (The mad disco strobe lighting.) We plough on. Bring out the trees and branches; let them litter the roads! The Gods must have crossed their arms in satisfaction, especially at the sight of me, completely drenched, hopping in and out of the car in the dark, hauling fallen branches to one side of the road, before another blinded driver was about to run me over.

'Maybe I should have stopped in Bergerac for petrol,' mutters Gerry as the petrol gauge stubbornly shines a bright red light. We make it to our friends' house in the nick of time. Luckily, Ian and Linda had insisted that we stay the night at their house, guessing correctly that we would be tired and hungry and talking gibberish. Also, wet and stinky. They were right and we are. Linda has thoughtfully bought two BIBs of Amblard wine. Linda says sagely: 'That'll be your breakfast sorted.'

Jesus, Mary, Joseph and the wee donkey – we are *here*! Home, home on the range where the ducks and the sunflowers grow! Except, now they don't. It is as if the duck farm had never existed. Instead, there is a field of ripening wheat. Mr Duckman has well and truly retired and sold his land to Mr Sunflowerman, who has decided this year to plant wheat instead of sunflowers.

It's been a whole year since we were last in this house. Nothing had been closed up properly and there is a definite stench of *foostiness*. The mice have come and gone after a whole year of carousing and refused to take their debris with them. Why do mice have a "field day"? Why not a "house year"? No matter what we do, this will always be a house in the middle of a field. I see a massive toad, like two hands clasped together, sitting gnome-like beside the door, as if welcoming us home. A delicate filigree of a recently spun spider's web hangs above my bed. I disturb two lizards finishing off the food on our plates inside the washing up bowl in the sink. This is the first time I have ever known lizards to spend any time in the house; they are always on the hunt for insects and the sun, clambering up the stony walls. They look surprised at our presence, as if to say, 'Why are you back?'

The old dishwasher has given up the ghost; the TV has conked out (after a few days it miraculously revives itself) and the new toilet refuses to flush – how contrary. Just as well we have driven down, since our car here has failed its *Contrôle Technique*, the equivalent of the MOT. It is languishing in the same Citroën garage we bought it from. The last car we took there was declared *bien foutu*, well and truly fucked. The worry is that this car will elicit the same response. At last, the Citroën car is fixed after three weeks – at a cost of €1500 – and passes the *Contrôle Technique*.

I discover that our local supermarket, *Intermarché*, is not one big company but a franchise. There must be a tax dodge somewhere in this. We had bought groceries from the *Intermarché* in Agen, only to find that the onions were off, and the mushrooms were overly fungied. A few days later I took the offending items back to the local *Intermarché* with the receipt. The check-out person turned up her nose and said, 'but why didn't you eat the mushrooms in the first two days?' I answered meekly that I didn't seek a refund just a replacement. The supervisor came round and explained that their *Intermarché* had nothing to do with the *Intermarché* in Agen and we would just have to return to Agen, a trip just short of an hour's drive. These are the minutiae of life that can drive you wild. Only in France can you turn on the radio and hear Boney M, Gary Glitter and anything from the *années yéyé*, the 1960s. To be fair, Serge Gainsbourg and Jane Birkin can go a long way.

Burglars have broken into the garage and stolen the 'John Deere' lawnmower. There is little else to steal, and the wasps' nest suspended like a lantern from the centre of the garage may have deterred them. Remarkably, there has been little water ingress. This is indeed a solid house. Days of airing and cleaning ensue. Gerry picks up the hammer where he left it a year before on the table and starts to make cupboards in the barn. I hack away at the dead white roses that have covered the window. The window is streaked with slug debris.

I had spent so long making a driveway the year before, and now there are hardly any stones to show for such backbreaking effort. My lapidary zeal had been a waste of time. A university lecturer once wrote this comment at the bottom of an essay I submitted: "You have covered more than you have mastered". How many times has this phrase come back to haunt me? *Festina lente* (more haste, less speed) should be my motto. I vow to slow right down, which will not be difficult in a place where the pace of life is usually slow, in any event. We do not anticipate any visitors. There should be a respectful time of "decontamination". Many French are suspicious of vaccinations and only fifty per cent of the population are vaccinated. There is a huge publicity drive to persuade people to come forward.

Our friends here have organised our social life. Our work is cut out. Lunch is brought out in the enamel cups with lids which we brought back from China. True workers' fare. Simon has been busy in our absence, hewing out an enormous terrace at the back of the house. We had tended to avoid the field at the back. There had been nowhere to sit out and besides, the wafting smell of duck guano was never very far away. 'Maybe one day we will have a swimming pool?' I ask Gerry brightly, and we howl with laughter.

Get the tambourines and nose flutes out! The Euros are upon us! We were last living in Aquitaine when the World Cup was on, and France won the title in 2018. Amazingly, after twenty-three years in the wilderness, Scotland is back in the game. The first game against the Czech Republic is a disaster, a defeat of two-nil. The build-up to the oldest football rivalry in the world, Scotland v England, in a sodden Wembley, sends jitters through us. As they say, it's not the size of the dog, it's the fight in the dog. We watch the match with our friends Norma and Iain, getting suitably *bluitered*. The two-all draw means that both sides can hold their heads up high. Then, of course, comes Scotland's inevitable defeat to Croatia. We continue to watch the matches in France and pick up on the French commentary: '*Ah, ils ont perdu leur mojo, ah, encore un corner...*' But it is '*bye bye les Bleus,*' as France is defeated. Defeat is met with *pah*, a shrugging of the shoulders and spit on the ground. There is a hint of defiance on the board outside the cheese shop:

Ici au moins
Les Bleus
Sont excellents!
Roquefort
Gorgonzola

The list goes on. (Here, at least, the blue cheeses are excellent: Roquefort, Gorgonzola...)

Our friends, Nicola and Robert, arrive from London. They are just in time for the Denmark v England match in the semi-final. Hunkering over stew on individual tables, the fire lit (it is unseasonably cold), we are transfixed by the TV for this momentous occasion. Gerry is ready with his home-fashioned horns sticking out of his head à la Shrek. The English fans boo the Danish national anthem, and a laser pen is directed at the eyes of the Danish goalkeeper, letting in the winning goal for England. The crowd erupts with jubilation, this, on the home turf of Wembley!

There are noticeably far fewer tourists in Aquitaine from Britain than usual. Our friends, Ron and Janet, ask us to look through the post that has been lying in their postbox for the last year. Snail mail is so called for a reason. The snails have managed to slowly macerate most of the letters into a slimy mush. The sultry actress, Rita Hayworth, famously used to tear up all the letters that arrived in her house. When someone pointed out that she may well be destroying cheques, she answered that there were bills there as well, so it evened everything out.

Parisians are starting to buy houses in the area en masse. Covid has persuaded city dwellers that a place in the countryside is de rigueur. The British *gîte* owners complain that their French visitors expect to have French TV available in the accommodation. This seems to me a perfectly reasonable expectation.

***

After three postponements to his wedding with Joanna, Ziggy, my son, at last was to be married on 3 July 2021 in Sydney. As much as we would have loved to have joined them, there was no way to breach the strict Australian Covid policy of not letting in outsiders. Indeed, there had been comparably few Covid cases in Australia. A couple of days before the wedding, there was a spike in infection. New South Wales was completely shut down, in the same way as had happened in the rest of Europe at the beginning of the pandemic. Poor Ziggy and Joanna – one day that knot will be tied! It's been two years since we saw them last when they visited us in Coutal, before embarking on their big Australian adventure in the football world. At least our eventual reunion will not be as long a wait as my father's was when he eventually met up with his mother after seventeen long years. War, and the consequences of war, had separated them for all this time. The first thing my father said upon meeting his beloved mother was, 'Oh, you have grown so old!'

***

Despite the pandemic, the local villages look fairly prosperous. Maybe there was nothing else to do but gardening and building work. 'All I did was zip up loads of outfits on my sewing machine,' says Jennie. Covid has been a blessing in disguise for one lucky restaurant that had ticked "pandemic" on their insurance form just before the disaster hit. Some businesses have gone under, unsurprisingly. Our local *boulangerie* has closed down. Who will now feed the *distributeur* in the village? Who will deliver our daily bread/croissants? When will we stagger up the drive with baguettes stacked like firewood under our arms?

The weekly market is still held in the villages. A stalwart since 1269, although people are wearing facemasks in spite of being outside. The mayor of our nearest village, whom I have known since I was twelve years old, has retired, and there is now a lady mayor, *Madame le Maire*. One is tempted to give her name a feminine equivalent, but the *Académie Française* would never allow such a faux pas.

The big event is that all the houses have now been numbered. So, at last we can be located by GPS. All the lanes have been given names. It is all official and bureaucratically satisfying. It is also confusing. The numbers are not sequential and, after asking a few neighbours, it seems that the number, say, 162, means that the house is 162 metres from the nearest road. It proves far more complicated than this. Something about the longitude and the latitude fed into an algorithm. No one quite understands the logic. Dutifully, we turn up to the *Mairie* to receive our official piece of paper to say we are the rightful residents of said house, at said address with a new number. It is a different number from the one we received last year. Maybe this is a code to give to aliens to easily detect us when they fall out of the sky.

We flag down the tractor cutting down all the wheat in the nearby fields and persuade the handsome chap to continue chopping down the ever-invasive bramble bushes around our property. The jungle is being tamed, and the lavender bushes carefully retained. The chap's father is Mr Sunflowerman, who has now bought the duck farm. Mr Sunflowerman Junior solemnly promises that I will no longer have to put up with *eau-de-canard* in my twilight years. Simon explains to me the next day, as he works on helping to build the terrace at the back, 'Oh you're out with the strimmer now, why is that?' I'm hacking away furiously at the undergrowth that's sprung up around the house.

I reply lasciviously, 'I'm finishing what the young lad has started.'

It's strange: no ducks, no *fouines*, no *loirs*, no stink, no bird scarer going off every few minutes and, for the moment, no mosquitos. In the middle of the night, I am in the toilet when, hark, I hear something gnawing away in the cupboard. It's a faintly reassuring rodent sound. Who needs perfection?

It's the end of the English dream of winning the World Cup. A gaggle of us have gathered together chez Linda and Ian for food, wine, chat and, surreptitiously, to sneak a look at the TV to check how well Italy and England are playing. Just five minutes before the end of the match, an electric storm hurls down its almighty force and the TV stops working. Panic ensues, a national tragedy.

Our mission this time is to concentrate on the barn and install our kitchen there, *un coin cuisine*. It seems that Gerry has been practising for his pièce de résistance – the kitchen – for many years. There has been barely a year that has passed where he has not installed a kitchen, either for us, relatives or friends. I reassure him that this will definitely be the last kitchen, before the next one. A magnificent beam has been salvaged and when we have smoothed it down, it will be used as a bar counter. Other smoother pieces of wood have been found, the grain beautifully polished, which unfortunately are far shorter than the length required. It takes some time to realise that they formed part of the byre, and the smoothness is by dint of cows rubbing up against the wood for many decades. Gerry and Nicola spend many happy hours debating what constitutes *the* perfect kitchen.

Nothing much has happened to change the bucolic rhythm of life here. The people we know are still around. At the age of eighty-one, Sue Castello, of the Pussy Galore voice, has sold her home and moved into a caravan. It's a temporary measure, as she has bought a complete wreck of a house in a nearby village with one of her seven children and her family. When they eventually receive the necessary permission, they will start building two dwellings. Ever optimistic, Sue thinks she will be able to move into her new nest in the spring. Outdoor life is fine for the moment, but winter can be brutal. I worry that she will be found in a frozen ball wrapped around her cat.

There is, however, one lucky *sleekit* duck called Jean-Pierre who has successfully managed to avoid the chop. The Gougets, our neighbours, are still going strong in their nineties and invite us to the usual banquet of home-produced delicacies.

They update us on the antics of Jean-Pierre, before filling us in with the local gossip. It is the first time (apart from the dogs), we have ever heard them name one of their animals. Jean-Pierre is a wild duck, a mallard, who somehow escaped the slaughter. His lady friend was not so lucky. She, we realise with dismay, is now the pâté served up in front of us. The survival instinct has kicked in with Jean-Pierre and he has ingratiated himself into the good books of Suzanne and Étienne, letting himself be patted on the head and waiting respectfully on the doorstep. He also hangs out with the chicks and the hens and insists on being locked up in the hencoop at night with them. One of the truffle hunting dogs, Coco, died recently, and maybe this duck has somehow lightened the burden of grief. Bibi, the other spaniel, is still alive but as deaf as Étienne. Étienne asks the whereabouts of Rocco. He sympathises that Rocco cannot join us since his European passport is no longer valid because of Brexit. We reassure him that our hound is safe and well in Scotland.

I unsuccessfully try to translate an old Bob Monkhouse joke: 'A vet and taxidermist have opened up a shop together with the tagline "Either way you get your pet back".' The thought of stuffing your dead pet and displaying it in your home is a strange conceit to these farmers. Étienne looks suitably puzzled. I try again, out of desperation. 'A young friend, just turned fifty years old, has recently married a man thirty years her senior. Gerry turns to her and says, "I bet you feel old age creeping up on you." Then, rather tactlessly, he looks at her older husband and then back at her and adds, "But I bet you know what that's about."' Étienne shrugs his shoulders and gives a look to Suzanne which says, *they are totally bonkers.*

There have been a few concessions to old age. Étienne seems frailer and Suzanne now needs a wheelchair and a walking stick. They can no longer drive their car, which makes them hostages in the countryside, reliant on children or neighbours to fetch and carry provisions. They have also decided that, along with the rabbits and the cows, the sheep have to go. They are just too much work. It looks like all that will be left of sentient beings will be Jean-Pierre and the poultry. Suzanne tells us that Parisians are buying up the houses all around. No doubt city life is not as attractive as it once was. She also tells us that out of the five nurses that come round to care for them, only one has been vaccinated. They might be growing old, nearly centenarians, but there is no problem with Étienne and Suzanne's reflexes as they expertly swat one fly after the other with the *plaquette* – the fly swatter. They take no prisoners. They resolutely refuse to contemplate the possibility of ending up in the old folk's home. As Étienne puts it, '*il n'y a qu'une seule sortie.*' There is only one exit.

The TV is turned on for Macron's presidential address, chastising the nation for wimping out of their duty. In two weeks time (August 2021), Macron intones, if you want to go to a café, restaurant, cinema or venue, you have to show the proof that you have had the double *jag*. Moreover, you will also need your *pass sanitaire* to travel on trains, planes and coaches. Then came the coup de grâce: by mid-September, all those who refuse to be vaccinated will be sacked from their jobs. The *chef d'état* is also taking no prisoners in *l'hexagone* as he refers to France. The message is clear, the measures draconian; the economy is about to go down the tubes if something drastic is not done. After all, it took two hundred years and a worldwide vaccination programme to eliminate smallpox. Macron even manages to squeeze in threats of raising the retirement age. The last time he did this, the gilets jaunes came out onto the streets protesting en masse. The response is immediate: over 9,260 people sign up to be vaccinated. Just to show that no one can deprive the French of their favourite pastimes. The sacrosanct holiday month of August is round the corner.

Étienne shakes his head and says, apropos of nothing, '*Il est jeune notre président*,' – our president is young – and switches channels to our favourite karaoke programme that is on at the same time every day, *N'oubliez pas les paroles! – Don't forget the words!* – which has a comforting Eurovision feel of inanity.

A few days later, we return their hospitality, inviting the Gougets and Madame Birot for lunch. Huguette Birot had originally sold Coutal Haut to my father in 1973 in order to build a tobacco barn. The last time I had met her, about thirty years ago, she was a sturdy, muscular farmer with short, grey curly hair and a ready smile that revealed a gold tooth that glinted in the sun. She had been living with her son in her retirement, but after her husband's death, at ninety years of age, she had decided to come back home and bought a cottage in a nearby village.

When I pick up the Gougets in my car, they are already at the door, in their best clothes, clutching a bottle of home-made *eau-de-vie*. Suzanne takes out a comb and gives Étienne a final scoop through his hair, spitting into her handkerchief to paste some strands onto his pate. After we have managed to shove all the crutches into our car and our visitors have negotiated the few steps into the house, the business of gossip is the order of the day. The ailments of others, Scrabble, the incomers, what local farmers are up to, how easy farming is now with all the mechanisation. 'Everything done by the touch of a button,' says Suzanne sniffily.

'Yes,' adds Étienne, 'these young farmers don't know what it's like to do a proper plum harvest, what backbreaking work that was.' They all sigh at the recollection.

Huguette had cared for an old couple, Mikael and Angèle, who had lived in Coutal Haut until their deaths and, as they had no children, they had left the house to Huguette and her husband. The house had remained empty from 1948 until my father had bought it twenty-five years later. 'And the bed Mikael slept in was just there.' Huguette points to the far end of what is now the through-room where we are presently sitting. 'The picture of the Madonna, the one that now hangs over the mantelpiece in the living room, used to be there over the bedstead,' she continues. She casts an eye over the barn. 'What happened to the hayloft, the byres for the seven cows, all the beams?' she asks. We discover that the French word for a stall is *crèche*, beautifully carved. A word that makes you feel that the cows – *les blondes d'Aquitaine* – were being well taken care of.

It looks like passers-by had just helped themselves to what they wanted from Coutal Haut. There were ruined houses everywhere when my father first came to Lot-et-Garonne. Now, in a weird twist of fate, the town not far away, Eymet, has been bought up by incoming Parisians as the English pack up and return home. A fitting reflection of the Hundred Years' War, when it would to and fro from being English, then French, then back again.

Huguette had helped the old man who owned the Château de Scandaillac, Monsieur Bonnefoi, with his pigeons and had been very fond of him. In return, he allowed her to hold her wedding in the château. This later followed the same pattern and fell into ruin once Monsieur Bonnefoi died. 'Ah, oui,' Huguette says softly, '*j'ai toujours aimé bien les vieux.*' I always liked old people. Then she turns to me. '*Et votre père, quel homme gentil!*' What a nice man your father was! I am taken aback. Very few people remember my father. They take bets on who will live to their hundredth birthday.

'*Après tout*,' says Suzanne, '*on est seulement que de passage ici.*' We are only here for a brief time on this Earth. As Robert Burns wrote in "Tam O'Shanter":

And like the snow melts in the river, a moment there
and gone forever.

'*À la santé à tout le monde, ici et dans le passé!*' To the good health of everyone here and those in the past! We toast those here and those departed with the walnut wine I had made two years ago with Suzanne's recipe. They all nod their approval. '*C'est si bon.*' Suzanne asks me to bring in some walnuts from the tree to test whether the nuts are ready for more winemaking, but they do not pass the quality assurance test yet.

Huguette invites us to her home to peruse some old photographs of me and my family some fifty years ago. My father is there. At one time, he was a photographer and so there are few photos of him, as he is the one usually behind the camera. In the photos, we are all dressed in our Sunday best. My white dress does not stand a chance; soon there will be some blotchy stain. One of my socks has fallen down. I vaguely remember having spent the morning climbing trees. One photo shows us all in front of the derelict Château de Scandaillac, a large sign on the gate warning us to keep out. When did falling masonry ever deter us?

There is a picture of Mikael, outside Huguette's house, ready to leave for war. The photo is a keepsake for his wife, Angèle. Presumably, it is 1914. He stands erect, clutching his gun and bayonet. His face is proud and kindly, reminiscent of Salvador Dalí with his swirling moustache. He doesn't know that the war will last four years and so many of his compatriots will be killed. Wherever this soldier has been sent, he is one of the lucky ones who manages to come home. (The final toll will be nine million men killed in the trenches). I try to imagine them in this house, Mikael and Angèle, not roaming far. For thirty years, sitting side by side in this living room every evening. It's a comforting image. Huguette can't remember their surname, so I trawl the local graveyards to try and find a stone inscribed with Mikael and Angèle, but to no avail.

Huguette is spurred on to find more photos of me and family. There is only so much one can take of seeing photos of yourself as a spotty teenager, looking thoroughly disdainful. We roll up to Huguette's at 11am to be greeted with a serried rank of alcoholic drinks which we didn't have the heart to refuse. '*Il faut trinquer! Santé!*' laughs Huguette – you have to drink up! Cheers!

Blanche, our former neighbour, who has beaten the rest of them to the centenarian title, is ensconced in the local old folks home. There, she is known as the chief and cajoles the young things to liven up. We are not allowed to visit because of Covid restrictions, but I spot the back of her chignon through the window. She looks in good spirits.

***

After many pleading calls, our plumber comes over unannounced to fix the toilet. I phone our friends Carol and Ian to delay our rendezvous at the local café. 'The plumber is here fixing the *cludgie*; we will be slightly late.'

'I'm sorry, didn't quite catch that,' comes back the posh voice.

'*The* cludgie, *she is being fixed!*' I say slowly. Only to find it is not Carol; I have phoned the wrong number and another refined English lady (Charlotte) has answered. She has no idea who this *cludgie* person is.

'*A la recherche du vide perdu*,' quips Nicola, proud of her French *jeux de mots*. We are back to our old addiction: scouring the *vide greniers*, the upmarket car boot sales. So far, I am the winner with the pickings: an advertising board with a 1950's housewife beaming, "I smile because I have absolutely no idea what's going on!", a pair of ladies' bellows, two flares, a Lalique copy plant stand, a selection of French books, one with the apt title *Quand j'ai vidé la maison de mes parents – When I emptied my parents' house*. Oh, that day will come. The rain on Bastille Day, 14 July, did not deter me, Gerry, Nicola and Robert from a *triple vide greniers* attack, but it did the vendors, who failed to turn up because of the foul weather. British people grumble because French shops are shut on this hallowed day, regardless of whether they are big or small. The British do not understand that national holidays are not excuses for massive consumer fests. However, this has gone one step too far! All the events have been cancelled due to either Covid or the rain. Instead, we seek refuge in various cafés and walk around the village of St Pastour.

'This place has always had a creepy feeling about it,' says Robert. 'Probably it's to do with the massive Cathar massacre,' a fantastic tongue twister, 'which took place in the thirteenth century.' He points out the well in front of the church that Cathars were thrown down. There is no plaque or explanation to mark the event, perhaps because it was the Catholic Church that persecuted the Cathars. In an age when war and capital punishment were commonplace, the Cathars believed that no one had the right to kill any living thing. This meant too, that they eschewed eating animals; should this be "no chew the animal"? These beliefs were abominations to the medieval mind and so the Cathars had to be eliminated. It reminds one of the practice when a woman was accused of witchcraft and given the ducking stool treatment. If she drowned, she was innocent. However, if she did not, she was burnt at the stake. Those accused of being a Cathar or a witch did not stand a chance.

Complaints of our mild aches abound. Robert with his bloodshot eye, Nicola with her swollen lip due to an allergic reaction, Gerry with his gout and me with the clicky knee, seem miniscule in comparison. Only briefly, mind; after a half-hour respite, we resume our moans. Robert reminds us that his father had been one of the original members of South-West Left, a group of British socialists in the 1980s who debated left-wing ideals from the comforting bosom of second homes in France. Our friend, Ron, was kicked out for being too left wing. So, it comes as a surprise when, soon after, on naming our quiz group "The South-West Lefties", as a laugh, a serious-looking gentleman at the next table comes up to introduce himself as the president of the South-West Left. He continues to explain that the group meet up every second month to debate liberty, egality and fraternity. If we want to know more about this august band, we only need to look up the British Embassy website under British communities in France. Henceforth, we and our fellow quislings, or rather, quizlings, Jill and Simon, will be known as "The South-West Lefties", a splinter group, a new undercover cell. Here's hoping that we are not met with the persecution meted out to the Cathars or witches.

Jennie and Ron, our friends from Château de Thomazeau in Castillonnès, have organised a book launch for me to promote my first book which was published earlier in the year. It will take place over two days in their courtyard with a restricted, spaced-out audience. Not so spaced out, quite lucid in fact. Covid has scuppered all the launches which had been arranged and any literary planning. This makes it perfectly apposite that the first official launch takes place in the area and home I write about. Happily, the local bookshop in Monflanquin has agreed to stock my book. Serendipity strikes: the sun comes out and the wine flows. I bring two platters of local Charlotte strawberries; the books are sold; the water from the fountain tinkles; and Jennie creates a banquet fit to launch all books. The only shadow is of my former self; I have worn my third choice of dress. The other two ripped at the sides as I pulled them on. To say I am well ripped is a misnomer, but I need to cut out the cheese and wine. Nevertheless, that is for cold turkey time, back in Glasgow, which will come soon enough.

It's difficult to stop Gerry from working. He is on a mission to finish as much as he can on his own. One evening, I find him at the back of the house hauling beams to an upright position against the wall. He explains that it is better that the beams are upright than flat on the ground, because it saves them from further weather damage.

After much nagging, we have found a way to keep the wooden ladders my father made in the barn. We have covered one internal wall in cedarwood. I am constantly inhaling the heady smell, as I walk past. We have a new favourite building merchant store, Leroy Merlin. For a long time, I thought this was written *Le Roi Merlin* (it's certainly pronounced that way), King Merlin. I was always puzzled by the reference to the Knights of the Round Table. On one foray, I spied a decent-sized elephant sculpture which would fit in perfectly with the quirky decor. *Be still my beating heart*, I thought before whisking Gerry over to view it. 'I'm afraid not,' came the verdict, 'its trunk is fine, but the legs are *squee-wiff*.' Yet again, another elephant dream dashed.

The only time we invite friends round is to celebrate the "raising of the bar". Albeit, as is our wont, the bar is at a slight slope. Old beams are never straight, after all. One must be wary of slipping glasses! Once, after an inebriated evening at our friend Kim's, I suggested that we play the James Bond game. 'What do you mean?' asked Gerry, warily.

'It's easy,' I explained. 'I pretend to be Rosa Klebb and ask how you want your Martini served, and you can be James Bond and that is when the bar comes in...'

But Gerry was having none of it and was horrified to find out that I had tried to balance on top of the bar. 'You could have killed yourself, next it will be pole dancing!' he yelled. He then conceded. 'OK, next time I'll be Parker and you can be Lady Penelope.' He shrugged his shoulders wearily.

'Promise?' I asked.

'Yes, milady,' he answered.

Although this is a gourmet's paradise, we have tended to avoid restaurants. One evening, we meet up with friends for a meal at the night market at Monflanquin. Nicola reassures us, 'Don't worry, it was very quiet last week, hardly anyone here, and it's outside, of course!' It is heaving, at least three hundred people in the market square, complete Covid central with people not wearing masks and elbowing each other. We are so unused to going out, that this is the second time we have forgotten our *couverts*, our plates, cutlery and glasses.

For years, we have been visiting the vineyard Clos la Coutale, not only because it has the best Cahors wine but also because it appeals to our vanity that our house has nearly the same name, and we can produce bottles of Coutale wine at the dinner table to our guests with a smirk. 'Fancy the house red?' We are delighted to discover that for years, unbeknownst to us, there has been lurking a gem of a restaurant, Le Caillau, just minutes' walk away from the vineyard, so we book a friends get-together with Linda, Ian, Simon and Jill. We are so loud and stay so long that we are eventually shooed off the premises. The food is *miam miam* and the tongue twister of the day is "Fleet Foxleys".

Our neighbour, Anthea, has been confined to a wheelchair of late. Her husband Bill has had to look after her and keep the *gîte* business going. She was overjoyed when her two children, Harriet and Justin, could at last visit after a two-year gap. We all met up at their house for a very French reunion. The conversation jumped from tales of Madame Claude and Régine of the Parisian sensual world to the mitochondrial DNA significance of sunflowers. Harriet brought out the beautiful sculptural remains of the hunter wasps, which had landed on mouldy books and spun their magic. Anthea noticeably perked up.

Christine and Patrick from across the road are selling up their beautiful guesthouse, the Moulin de Labique. The new owner, might, just might, open a restaurant. Imagine – we can walk to food made by others!

Our last memorable banquet was at Tracey and Ken's. This was an Indian feast, just before we left. One of the guests told me a barn had burnt down that morning near where they lived. Three fire engines whizzed up the track to extinguish the flames, hotly pursued by a service vehicle. The personnel leaped out of the last vehicle, brought out tables and chairs, covered the table with tablecloth and flowers, and a first-class meal was laid out ready for the firefighters when they had done their business.

I fully intended to do my thirty days yoga course on my computer. However, I have made slow progress. I did Day One on the first day here and Day Two on the 27th. God knows when Day Three will emerge.

I wake up in a panic. I dream, not of firefighters – the best dream – but that I have acquired a deck, a patio, a terrace and a veranda. I can no longer remember the difference between each one or recall under which extension I have buried Gerry.

Eleven

Sharon in Smithereens *Swanlights*

You are everywhere in this house; you permeate its walls; you wrap your arms around us all. All the things that belonged to you: the Provençal dressers, photographs, candlesticks, lamps, carpet, plates, the candelabra we bought in an antique shop in Prague. '*Bohemian* glass, how divine,' I hear you say. Your posthumous present from the three sisters, the metal silhouettes of boxing hares, are waiting to be placed in the optimum place in the garden. These came about after one of the comedian Janey Godley's video clips of boxing hares screaming abuse and hitting each other while screeching, 'Christiana, you watch my eyelash extensions, I just fucking got them this week...' In homage, your eyelash extensions are stuck over the animals' eyes.

'There,' said Eunice with satisfaction, 'a bit of Sharon's DNA.'

Your spirit floats around, dressed in tartan, dancing and singing. 'Fill up your glass; let's have some music! How about Leonard Cohen's last offering? Some like it darker... you hit the light?' We sit outside watching the stars twirl, sipping wine, listening to music.

> Hobgoblin nor foul fiend, shall daunt her spirit
> She knows that she at the end, shall life inherit.
>
> (adapted) John Bunyan

You first came here when you were nineteen, stick thin with a perm. Our friend Hugh teased you relentlessly. Once, in Biarritz, you were stopped by police for sleeping on the beach. You pointed to Hugh and said, 'I'm with him,' and Hugh shrugged the nonchalant Shuggie shrug and said he'd never met you before in his life. Then you had a showdown in La Bulle nightclub in Monflanquin. A few years later, you sang "The Lord's My Shepherd, I'll Not Want" in Queen's Chapel in Belfast for Hugh and Bronagh's wedding. Bronagh says people still ask about the girl who sang so beautifully at her wedding.

You were such a fusspot, a complete dilettante. You loved beauty, music, literature, travel, ribald stories, joy in life, your children, sisters, friends, profundity, profanity and your constant projects. You hated bores, bananas, dried tomatoes, avocados, purple prose and pomposity.

There is a photo stuck to the fridge. Our friend Liana is exultant. She is sitting in the middle of us on the sofa showing off her gold bra, her red lipstick glistening, and we are laughing, heads back, mouths open.

'What would Sharon say?' we ask when faced with some ridiculous situation, knowing full well the answer.

The Kalahari bushmen trek vast distances across the desert. 'When we die, we die,' they say. 'The wind blows away our footprints and that is the end of us.' I dread such finality.

Grief snakes in and out of my body, seeking out a weak spot, like a Covid variant. To me, you are alive and present in my heart. Rosemary sent over a Lancaster rose in a pot on the day of your funeral. I wish you could see it, Sharon. It is blooming, so many deep red roses.

You bought a visitors' book for us and wrote: "A haven of heat, sleep, wine and best friends. Bliss. I love this place. Xxxx".

You coveted the paintings of Heather Nevay. Once, we nearly bought the one with the shapeshifter's theme, with a leather mask and a huge, hooked nose, like one who sniffed out plague victims (just like in Mary King's Close) with a bird lurking inside the body.

Are you hiding here, somewhere, in another guise? The frenetic beating of the swan wings? The light glinting from their feathers?

My heart aches.

Why did you leave so soon?

I light a candle for you, here, in your resting place. This is your home too.

Si l'on me presse de dire pourquoi je l'aimais, je sens que cela ne se peut exprimer qu'en répondant: 'Parce que c'était elle, parce que c'était moi.

If you pressed me to say why I loved her, I can say no more than because she was she, and I was I.

Twelve

July & August 2021
Inside and Outside World

Ach, I know, we are the jovial ones.

The mice are bored. They are paring their claws, insouciant, eyeing up the house. It will not be long before they are back to mouse party time.

It's time to go. France has been declared an "amber plus" country by Britain, which means we have to leave ten days earlier than anticipated, so we can quarantine for that number of days on arrival in Glasgow. We must be fresh and raring to return to work the next day. I clear out the garage, evicting all the rodent tenants, having come up with the novel idea of parking our French car there. Why hadn't we thought of that earlier? One last smash and grab at Villeréal market to stock up on boxes of Amblard wine, tins of pâté and plaits of garlic. I leave some on the floor of the barn and Gerry tells me that he spies a mouse around. Or as he says, "a moose aroon". 'Then they are the very rare breed of vampire mice,' I answer.

I was curious to know why the first thing Emmanuel Macron did on becoming President in 2017 was to visit the village of Oradour-sur-Glane in Aquitaine. The village has been preserved in its ruined state after the massacre of 642 men, women and children. This, as a memorial to the cruelty of the Nazi occupation in World War Two. Macron's appearance was to underline the "never again" message, as a warning about the rise of right-wing extremism. It is the beginning of the new Covid requirements, and we manage to provide a passable *pass sanitaire*, which is a mandatory requirement for entry into any museums and other institutions.

Oradour-sur-Glane is certainly a powerful reminder of the horrors of war. It's quite a large village, more a town, that testifies to a certain prosperity: solidly built houses with central heating radiators and a large variety of shops, bars and cafés (the café Brandy caught my eye), restaurants, post office, garages, a large hotel and three schools. Tangled metal, mostly burnt-out cars, are all that's left. As the tram line runs directly to nearby Limoges, Oradour-sur-Glane was essentially a latter-day commuter belt suburb. Wandering around the ghostly ruins with the names of what the buildings once were: tobacconist, hardware store *inter alia*, as well as the names of the proprietors. Later, in the museum, gazing at the photographs of those murdered, one is constantly reminded that they were just ordinary people leading ordinary lives. Just like the photos of all those killed in Gaza on the front cover of the *New York Times*. Just like the photos of *los desaparecidos*, the young people killed in Argentina's dirty war in the 1970. The futility of war hits with full force. The surnames on the 1914–18 war memorial in the church in Oradour are the same surnames as those who had lost their lives in yet another act of barbarity, only one generation before. Approximately, sixty million people died in World War Two, for what? A better, safer world?

There were a few things that troubled me, as I walked through the exhibition. One of the first exhibit panels talks about the resistance in Nazi Germany. As if exonerating the Germans in World War Two for their guilt should be the focus. For sure, not all Germans were Nazis, but all Nazis were German, and they were in the majority. Fear too, is a factor in silencing those who disagreed. Nevertheless, silence is complicity of sorts if what has happened is in your name. Many of those in the SS corps were from the annexed French regions, mainly Alsace, and were young, approximately eighteen years old. They were already brutalised, having been involved in previous massacres in the area. Of the 642 people killed in Oradour, only fifty-two could be identified. Corpses were so badly mutilated and burnt. What horrifies me is the zeal of someone so young who could inflict such terrible acts. Most of the SS division of two hundred were killed in the subsequent Normandy campaign and no one was held accountable at the time for what happened. What is so shocking, incomprehensible and ironic, is to discover that the emblem of the 2nd SS Panzer Division Das Reich, i.e. those responsible for the massacre in Oradour-sur-Glane, is the same emblem adopted by the Ukrainian Azov Division fighting in the Donbass region in Ukraine today. The evil shadow of Nazism has somehow infiltrated this nightmare.

After the war, a trial was held in Bordeaux of twenty-one men accused of perpetrating war crimes in Oradour-sur-Glane (of those sixty-five still alive). Just twenty were found guilty. This caused such a huge uproar in Alsace that, eventually, the fourteen Alsatian former SS men found guilty were released.

An amnesty was declared by the French parliament for those who had been coerced into fighting for the Germans. This was because their region had been annexed. I had not realised that such a large area in France was under the Vichy Government, the collaborationist regime. Thus, the shame and guilt of French complicity is a sebaceous layer, resurfacing when lightly scratched. Apparently, less than one per cent of the French population were in the resistance.

Most of Aquitaine was in the occupied part of France and there were many similar massacres. They were described as "ordinary" massacres, those "run of the mill" massacres that took place all over Eastern Europe, where no one was deemed ultimately accountable. There was only a passing mention of the slaughter in the rest of the continent.

Displayed on the floor of the museum are moral epithets such as:

Ceux qui oublient le passé se condamnent à le revivre

Georges Santayana

"Those who forget the past are condemned to relive it". Maybe this should be amended to: "Those who forget the present are condemned to relive it".

***

We arrive at the Channel Tunnel in Calais that evening and practise the tongue twister of the evening – Purring Past Paris – confident that we have all the necessary papers: PCR test results, passenger locator forms completed. One would have thought that the French are in their bureaucratic element, but *non*. We are taken in for questioning, redo the passenger form and cause a *stooshie* when we casually mention that we are in transit through England to reach Scotland. A supervisor is called over. 'So how are you going to get to Scotland through England?' She eyes us, suspiciously.

'We keep on driving,' we blithely answer.

'All the way? No ferry?' she persists. 'How can you prove you live in Scotland?' Who would have thought a Scottish bus pass, my Saltire Card, with my photo and the word "Glasgow" emblazoned on it, would come in so handy?

We are beckoned into the next area. The woman at the desk looks at me and says, 'What are you doing here? I have an emergency!'

'But we were told to come here,' we answer, confused.

'*Non, il ne faut pas s'énerver!*' Don't get annoyed! 'Can't you see how busy it is here?' The train is full! There are hardly any cars or passengers to be seen.

'*Mais je ne m'énèrve pas, Madame,*' I answer. I am not annoyed.

'*Il faut être calme!*' she screeches.

'But I am calm,' I say slowly. '*Je... suis... un... prof... du... calme.*'

At this, she goes completely ballistic and tells us to get out of her office. At passport control, I mention the scene to the smiling lady at the booth. 'Ah, yes. They are all having a breakdown because the authorities have insisted that the French port officials are now in charge of all Covid administration. This has tipped them over the edge.'

Meanwhile, bad juju comes our way. It may be the fact that I have accidently packed two shoes from different pairs or that I am so convinced that the weather is going to be *scorchio* in Scotland that I order two new sun loungers to be delivered to our Glasgow door. Suddenly, the car, a Vauxhall Zafira (like all our cars, bought second hand for around £1k), lost its power steering, a careless act in itself. Then the alternator goes kaput. Luckily, Gerry manages to steer the limping car off the motorway and stop at a service station. The AA breakdown service is promptly called, the car is tweaked; all to no avail. It is a Sunday, and we will have to wait till the following day for the repair garage to open.

Kettering for thirty hours. It sounds like the title for a sitcom. We are unexpectedly holed up in the motorway Travelodge. Intriguingly, Kettering is known for its manufacture of Weetabix and lesser known for the spyware company Pegasus. From cereal to links with the deep state.

Just by chance, we find a path that takes us over the bridge to Kettering, where we meander for many a distracted hour. Tracking down the *chemins de désir*, the paths of desire, is a favourite pastime of ours. We like finding the more favoured shortcuts made by local people, rather than following the designated signposts. Sunday in Kettering is a shut-shop affair and the few people we see are waiting outside the foodbank. 'Do you know the origins of the name Kettering?' asks Gerry. He proceeds to explain that ending "ing" denotes that it is from the tribe of, so Kettering means the "place of Ketter's people". Spontaneously, we try to think of other place names with the suffix "ing": Spalding, Hastings, Worthing, Goring, Angmering. Nothing tops the outburst of the near-blasphemous *Godalming*! We have recently played the same game with place names ending in "ac". In Aquitaine, also meaning "the place associated with", there are countless names to choose from: Ferrensac, Bergerac, Pompiac, Jarnac, Riberac, Dévillac for example. In the end, during this earlier game, we had to limit it to a thirty-kilometre radius of Coutal Haut.

Kettering is a pretty town, and our main diversion is drawing inspiration from the town to make up names for possible exhibitions. The more pretentious the better. It is, of course, the long-winded and tedious explanations accompanying the masterpieces that are the howlers. We take our lead from Joseph Beuys, the German artist. About ten years ago, Gerry and I went to a retrospective of his work. Were we philistines not to appreciate the wonder of his oeuvre? *Fat chair* was our favourite sculpture: a blob of fat on a kitchen chair. One was not enough. Later he made another sculpture with the fat built up into a triangular wedge on the seat of the chair. Fat, felt and honey were his favourite materials, as were his "Aktions" – performance events such as being cooped up with a coyote for a week or explaining art to a dead hare. His accompanying commentary is so good I am compelled to quote it here:

> *In putting honey on my head, I am clearly doing something that has to do with thinking. Human ability is not to produce honey, but to think, to produce ideas. In this way the deathlike character of thinking becomes lifelike again. For honey is undoubtedly a living substance. Human thinking can be lively too. But it can also be intellectualised to a deadly degree, and remain dead, and express its deadliness in, say, the political or pedagogic fields. Gold and honey indicate a transformation of the head, and therefore, naturally and logically, the brain and our understanding of thought, consciousness and all the other levels necessary to explain pictures to a hare: the warm stool insulated with felt... and the iron sole with the magnet. I had to walk on this sole when I carried the hare round from picture to picture, so along with the strange limp came the clank of iron on the hard stone floor – that was all that broke the silence, since my explanations were mute...*

Joseph Beuys

I read this again and tears of mirth are coursing down my face. Ah, the saturation of jargon!

In Kettering, we photograph many "shadows" of old

buildings which had presumably once been there; a door in the middle of a building suggests an outside staircase has been taken away; the apex of a roof is silhouetted against another building. The title of our proposed exhibition is called *Un train peut en cacher un autre* (one train can hide another), up to Beuys exacting standards, as is our own gobbledygook blurb:

> *A restaurant called Mystic Diners conjures up a surrealist concept of diners transmitting their culinary desires telepathically; "in this work of the three yakkers, combining nymphomaniac, kleptomaniac and mythomaniac, the diners sublimate their desires in their quest to satiate Rabelaisian appetites..."*

Basia Gordon & Gerry Coutts

This is followed by a series of closed windows with foliage peeking through which inspires another reverie. There is no limit to plumbing the depths of our artistic pretentions.

Sharon and I used to call times of complete introspection and obsession our "Morandi moments". The Giorgio Morandi exhibition in the Tate had been a complete revelation to us. Here was an artist so insular that he could block everything out to concentrate on his work. He lived all his life with, and was looked after by, his three sisters in the same family home in Bologna. Except for a brief foray to the World War One battlefields, where he was invalided out following a nervous breakdown. After that, he never strayed far from the confines of his Italian home. The main themes of his work were painting still lifes of bottles, vases and jugs. He went to bed for most of World War Two. It simply passed him by. His description of his work emitted howls of laughter from Sharon, along the lines of, 'Listen to this – "sometimes I move around the objects in a different configuration on the tabletop to create tension, which has me on edge for days on end". Again, I quote one of the jewels of art reviews:

> Giorgio Morandi: Resistance and Persistence
> Morandi, the priest of subversion and reverence, sits in his small room stroking his humble surfaces with a vibrating acceptance of the impossibilities and necessity of resistance. Resistance to the majority and resistance to progress. [His painting] wasn't exciting yet it was exciting. Exciting in its resistance, in its subversiveness.
>
> Sean Scully artcritical online magazine, 1/9/08

By this time, Sharon and I would be on the floor convulsed with laughter, kicking our legs up in the air.

It has been a long time since Gerry and I have had such enforced rest and easy chat. We batted an eyelid and Wimbledon passed us by. Now, in the comfort of our Travelodge, we can enjoy the highlights of the Tokyo Olympics on TV. The gymnasts with their plasticine bodies and the French winning the Fencing competition. *En garde*!

'Do you know, there are some things no one talks about?' I say to Gerry, pensively. 'What happened to Gadhafi's bodyguards?' They were called the Revolutionary Nuns. Young, good-looking women with sunglasses, glossy hair and make-up. The Western press called them the "Amazonians". They wore combat gear and carried guns. From the 1980s, they were constantly at the Great Leader's side. Gadhafi explained their presence by saying that he was safer with female bodyguards because would-be assassins would be reluctant to shoot women. Nothing to do with being a megalomaniac who loved to be surrounded by pretty women.

'They are probably raped or dead,' replies Gerry, deadpan.

'OK,' I counter. 'Then what do you think happened to the sign language interpreter at Nelson Mandela's funeral, who patently had no idea how to do sign language and was constantly trying to duck the sights of the TV coverage?'

'Fingers probably fell off,' answers Gerry. I sigh. Sometimes it's difficult to engage with the lad.

As soon as the car is fixed, we head north with one last tongue twister: Keeping cattle as a caper in Kettering.

***

4 August 2021. It's been one year since the explosion in Beirut, the biggest non-nuclear explosion in modern history. No one is held accountable; the usual lexicon appears: "scuffles and clashes". There has been political deadlock for the last year. My cousins, Sarah and Zeina, send texts filled with despair. Up to three hundred thousand Lebanese have left the country since 2019, including seventy per cent of all medical staff. The currency has lost ninety per cent of its value in two years. There are food shortages, forty-five minutes of electricity a day and corruption is endemic.

Later in the month, US and British troops pull out of Afghanistan and the country implodes. It is difficult to believe that more Americans have been killed in Iraq and Afghanistan (around ten thousand) avenging the three thousand or so who were killed in the New York World Trade Centre in 2001.

The arms companies must have had a field day.

***

The end of our ten-day self-internment back in Glasgow coincides with France being taken off the "amber plus" list and *la grande rentrée*, the return to school in mid-August. Nevertheless, these ten days give me food for thought. Since Sharon died, I have been increasingly aware of how precious time is, how it is not to be squandered. But how am I going to escape the treadmill of teaching? *Plus ça change, plus çest la même chose.* I have witnessed the full educational revolution in the last thirty years. There have been some wonderful times, like the last time I organised a school trip to my special place in Aquitaine just before the pandemic, and the pupils bought food from the markets and cooked for me and my colleague as well as visiting the prehistoric site of Lascaux and Joséphine Baker's château. *Miss, she is dancing naked!* Our local mayor happily entertained *les gosses d'Écosse* – the Scottish kids – in the *Mairie*. I add that no naked dancing took place. The parents were so thankful for such an 'authentic' school trip that they bought me French wine when we returned to Glasgow!

Nevertheless, I am becoming increasingly disgruntled and yearn for some fannying-around time. An incident happens just before the end of the summer term which crystallises my decision to leave.

***

I am older and I have lost my allure. I am in the photocopier room, waiting patiently for the two young teachers in front of me to finish doing what they are doing. They are in no hurry. They are discussing the book they studied at school, *To Kill a Mockingbird*, and their English teachers. 'Oh, my teacher was well past it, in her fifties, at least.'

I stand behind them. They don't see me, because I am now one of these invisible teachers. Shapeless, sexless, meaningless, well past her sell-by date; an ex-battery hen caged in a coop. Evanescence. The quality of vanishing and then being forgotten. The first time I visited the London Planetarium, I felt at first the joy, the sheer wonderment of the possibilities of endless universe and swirling stars. Then I was caught short by the realisation that we were all infinitesimal specks in the firmament. I was plummeted back to earth.

I want to give them my full Gloria Swanson moment in *Sunset Boulevard*. "I am big; it's the pictures that got small". (There's always a swan lurking somewhere in the background.)

I suspect I am the cuckoo in the council's "family". I don't understand most of the organisational acronyms anymore. I should invest in a hearing trumpet and pince-nez glasses, adopt a dowager's hump and wander around others muttering, 'Eh?' One acronym should be reintroduced: an old army term, SNAFU, meaning Situation Normal All Fucked Up.

Teachers nowadays sign off emails with the pronouns they want to be referred to by, e.g. he/him or she/her. I am tempted to sign with a flourish: *Majesty*.

Time to leave when you are told that you have to render the reports on pupils anodyne: say nothing about their progress, what your impression is of them, just outline the next steps. Gone are the days when I could write "Fernando is so laid back he's in danger of falling over". Besides, the rising numbers of 'ologies', my favourites being "'oppositional defiance disorder' and 'spirited children', were testing my roles as therapist, psychologist, nurse and entertainer, in addition to teacher.

The exit is in front of me. My former headteacher wrote 'some days are great – , but most are brilliant!". It is definitely the moment for me to *accrocher les patins*, to hang up my skates, to end this particular career and just be the boss of me, paddling my own canoe.

And maybe, at this moment, I have as much oomph left as a deflated old tyre. As they say in French, *je n'ai plus de nyac*.

Onwards to a positive destination. But how?

Foolishly, I had only started paying into my pension after I had the children. For the first ten years of teaching, there were few permanent jobs. Consequently, I was on temporary contracts all that time. Without maternity benefit and job security, there seemed little point in investing in a future so very far away. I was now a fully functioning, cynical sixty-year-old with arthritis in her fingers, healthy mortgage and the nirvana of the state pension constantly snatched from me by the government's changing rules. All the money we had gleaned in the last few years had been thrown, nay, chucked at the money pit that is Coutal Haut.

There *is* some way out of here! The lightbulb moment! We can sell the house in Glasgow, pay off our debts and live in the aforementioned tiny flat down the road. This is, after all, a seller's market, we are told. We might be stuck in the house for ten days, but at least we could crack on, pack up the house and give away furniture. A jury citation awaits me. It is with satisfaction that I can ask to be relieved of my civic duty by returning all the French paperwork to prove we have to do quarantine. Apart from that, teachers are now classed as essential workers.

Rocco, our hound, has returned to the fold and I take him for walks down the canal towpath. I spy a swan family, serenely gliding down the canal. Two adults and two sturdy teenagers, their dark down revealing glimpses of white. They have survived! Then I spy another swan nuclear family, in another stretch of the canal. Followed by two barges and then, heavens forfend, another identical swan family. I am amazed and perplexed – which ones are our swans?

***

Meanwhile, I still have to return to the chalk/screen face whilst the Great Escape plans are firmed up.

The *virelangues* posters – tongue twisters – that a class have made hang from the wall:

Seize chaises sèchent
(Six chairs drying)
Son chat chante sa chanson
(His/her cat sings its song)
Un taxi attaque six taxis
(A taxi attacks six taxis)
As-tu été à Tahiti?
(Have you been to Tahiti?)
Chouette chaussures
(Nice shoes)

Instead of discussing how to teach pupils wearing facemasks at a one-metre distance, thirty-three at one time crammed into a classroom with windows that barely open, we are treated to workshops on the "science of learning" and "why moderation is not verification". This reminds me of the old joke: "Got kicked out of my positive thinking class. It was shit anyway". I find comfort in a radio broadcast *The Power of Negative Thinking*. One woman reports her work as a companion to the dying in a hospice. She remarks that it isn't "the bucket list" that people mention at the end. It is simply a regret that they didn't stop to enjoy the simple pleasures in life, instead engaging in this hell-bent urge to cram in as much as possible.

There is always a point in pregnancy when you look down and can no longer see your feet, but you know that it will only be for a short while and then the pain will subside. Then there will be a new beginning. So it is with teaching. Once our cunning plan is activated, I too can be liberated. Like the swans, I look as if I am coping fine, but I am paddling furiously under the surface.

Samuel Pepys commented that every home in the seventeenth century had a very distinct smell. I can't say the same about ours in Glasgow: it smells of cleaning unguents and a vague whiff of hound. An upmarket toilet. It is also very bare; I am a maximalist who has had minimalism forced upon me. A friend suggested that we rent storage space as we prepare to downsize. We have already disembarked forty boxes into the facility, mainly books. After we move to the small flat, I can go and visit the boxes and stroke them lovingly. However, I fear that many possessions will eventually be jettisoned. Gerry has made it crystal clear that no item can be despatched to France. 'If it's in the wrong country, it's not going anywhere,' he threatens. It has taken us ten years to replace the skirting boards that Rocco chewed when he was a puppy. Now I feel I can lick them they are so new and clean. Our home looks eerily pristine now that it has been prepared for sale, "staged" and "dressed", denuded, bereft of character with walls repainted. All our personal objects have been surgically removed and plants and flowers have been shipped in, courtesy of my green-fingered Aunt Yvonne. It's time for someone else to take over this show home.

Thirteen

September & October 2021 *Inside World*

———————————————————

'What have you done with the toaster?' I ask Gerry, crossly. '*You have hidden the toaster!*' There is no end of all our worldly possessions disappearing. At the same time as we are titivating our house in Glasgow, my cousin Daniel and his wife Ellen, who have returned to live in in Taiwan, contact us. They ask us to arrange the handover of their nearby flat to new tenants, Taiwanese students. In all the kerfuffle, I have misplaced the flat keys and it dawns on me that I may well have packed them in a box which is now in the storage facility. I drag a reluctant and grumpy Gerry to our locker in the city centre. We proceed to go through all the recently delivered boxes, to no avail. Back home in the pouring rain, soaked in despondence and a cloak of gloom, I miraculously retrieve the keys from the bottom of a dish, just in time for two bedraggled Taiwanese students to arrive at the door. I resolve to be more organised.

Following the estate agent's advertisement, a constant

stream of would-be buyers traipse through our house. They come from all over: Berlin, Prague, Istanbul, Nigeria, Hong Kong, as well as the home-bred variety. The Hong Kong couple come to view twice, surprisingly. When they open a cupboard during the first viewing, at least ten annoyed bluebottles fly straight into their faces. We later discover that a tiny mouse has managed to squeeze in to partake of some of Rocco's food. After expiring from overeating and entering into mouse heaven, the bluebottles have feasted on its corpse. (This would be part of daily life in Coutal Haut.) The second time the couple visit is to check on the water pressure in the upstairs bathroom. At least this is what they tell us. Thankfully, there is no second disaster. No dribble, no torrent of water, not one fly to surprise them this time. No doubt they are also checking out our hygiene. As soon as each potential buyer leaves, either a barge or swan or kayak comes into view on the canal, but tantalisingly not into the view of the viewers.

The house sells within the week. I drag the boxes which had been temporarily stored in the car back into the house. They have been sheltering there whilst we display the emptiness which was our home. With a sigh of relief, I invite Fran and Jen, our fellow Schemies, as well as Yvonne and Eunice, to celebrate with champagne and supper. My mother has produced her home-made *pączki*, Polish doughnuts, stuffed with rose jam. They are the nectar of the gods; every part of the process she has done herself. The petals are picked from the roses growing near Ayr Beach, *eau-de-vie* added to the yeast. It is labour-intensive work.

Early in the morning, the swans emerge from the fog, sailing sedately by. Silently passing, as if to congratulate us. The two cygnets now sport white highlights on their down. They are growing up quickly.

The next day is a working day – we turn up, present but, without doubt, are unfit for work.

Yvonne, my mother's sister, is recovering from breast cancer and slowly regaining her strength. When I can, I take her out on trips, such as a visit to my friend Norma in Crieff. Norma's ebullient, acquisitive and fun-loving boyfriend, Iain, cannot stop himself from amassing big stately piles which Norma subsequently has to organise. 'I've got castle hassle,' sighs Norma wearily. 'That's why I've installed a chair in the lift, so I can have a rest. I walk miles of corridors a day.' It's a pleasant affliction for her to have, as far as her friends are concerned. We all get to enjoy the sumptuous, spacious surroundings. Iain's son and daughter-in-law have had two children during Covid, reasoning that they could just make their own people, as it is impossible to see others.

Autumn is gently stirring, and the leaves are turning colour. There is a Polish genetic stirring deep within me and Yvonne, as we walk in the Perthshire hills, picking one full-blown mushroom after another. Gerry arrives home from visiting his family in Lossiemouth, bringing a smell of wood smoke which mixes with the mushrooms drying in the oven, an olfactory feast. A week later, after dropping off copies of my book at Bridget's café in Tighnabruaich, Yvonne and I take Rocco for a walk along the Cowal Way. Every turn reveals a glorious vista of hill, loch, boats and islands. It is a beautiful day, warm and clear and midgie-free, and we meet no one. Despite his advancing years, Rocco cannot have enough of running in and out of the water fetching his ball, as Yvonne fills her chemo-hat (which usually covers her now hairless head) with chanterelles. Some opportunities cannot be missed! Back home, the house is saturated with smells of sautéed mushrooms and a deliciously seaweed-infused dog.

Slowly, everything is opening up again.

"Doors Open Day" is a rolling event which takes place every year around Britain. Annually, on this day, the public are allowed free access to buildings which are not usually open to the public. As part of this year's Doors Open Day, Yvonne and I visit the Alasdair Gray Archive in the nearby Whisky Bond, just up the canal. Gray's study in his West End flat, with all his eclectic belongings, such as writing desk and jam jars, has now been recreated and found a permanent home. He was a creative genius in word, line, brush and pen.

A confession. When Gray was going through one of his many impecunious moments, he was desperate to sell his art cheaply. I was fortunate enough to buy six original prints of his masterpiece, *Lanark*, which decorated my walls for over thirty-five years. When his luck changed and he became successful, he tried to contact me to buy them back. I resolutely refused and, in the end, gave them to my daughter Irena as an early wedding present.

The towpath on our canal has been developed and improved all the way down towards the city centre with "rewilding" sections and placement of artworks. One of the last of Alasdair Gray's works can be found there: a fusion of sculpture and poetry, stones carved with the following sayings:

THE FUTURE OF WILDLIFE DEPENDS ON
HUMANITY
THE EARTH, ON WHICH OUR OWN LIVES
DEPEND
FREEDOM IS FAITH IN DREAMS SUGGESTING
NEW GROWTH

IF WE CAN GLADLY USE IT
THE PRESENT IS OUR HAPPIEST GIFT.

One Doors Open Day is memorable in my mind. In 1997, Janey Buchan, a colourful and slightly eccentric MEP (Member of the European Parliament), an ex-Communist Party member who later joined the Labour Party, sent out an invitation stating that anyone was welcome to see the complete *guddle* in which she lived, surrounded by memorabilia and stacks of newspaper bundles. Most mornings, I would pass by her house on a hill on the way to taking Irena to primary school. It looked like a shambling heap, in need of an edifice lift. Given that this was Janey's home, only a few people would be allowed in. I was delighted to receive an invitation. I turned up at the allotted time on the specified day, only to find that the house was resolutely locked up. It was a Doors Shut Day. Puzzled, I wandered home through deserted streets. Much later, I received a note from Janey saying that, given it was the day of Princess Diana's funeral, she thought it only right and respectful to cancel the event and didn't think anyone would venture out on such a sad day of national significance. It would seem that even the staunchest of republicans have a soft spot for the royal family.

Back to the present and the TRNSMT festival holds sway in Glasgow for two days. This year it is very aptly named as Covid rips through the sweaty crowd of revellers. Liam Gallagher, erstwhile of Oasis, is the headline act and postures like a rebel. He has never done a rebellious thing in his life, apart from posing with Tony Blair in a photo shoot at No.10 in the Cool Britannia era.

***

Irena, my daughter, is catching up with all her friends' missed weddings for the last two years. We meet up for an afternoon in Dunkeld. It strikes me as odd that I have seen Sharon more recently than I have Irena. Even though Irena lives in London, the pandemic has effectively kept us apart for the last eighteen months. She is completely oblivious to the fact that I spent so much of my childhood in Dunkeld, as my Auntie Margaret (as well as her sister, Nan, now in Ecclefechan, and Janet in Beirut) came from a nearby village. She and my grandfather ran an antiques shop in the town square. Irena and her friends all pile into the car with a soggy Rocco lying over his humans and visit the Kinnaird Estate. Apart from one house that has fallen into disrepair, it is the same as it ever was. I think the last time I was here was for the reunion with the family from Beirut.

***

At last, I receive an appointment card to the anaphylaxis clinic for skin tests, a year after my latest hospitalisation in France. I am overjoyed to discover that I am only highly allergic to brazil and almond nuts and cannot wait to stuff my mouth with my beloved macadamia and pecan favourites. Not so fast. I notice that it is 3.15pm on the clock on the hospital wall. The next thing I remember is lying on a stretcher with my legs up, as the doctor tells me in a serious voice that my system was overwhelmed when they took a blood test. It is now 3.55pm. I had passed out and my pallor is grey and sweating. 'It is a vasovagal reaction,' says the doctor gravely. It sounds so important; I have a real "condition", something to be proud of. For the next hour, I remain prone, so my condition can be monitored. I start to fret that this might affect future nut consumption. How disappointing to discover that it was a mere common garden fainting episode that afflicts fifty per cent of people some time in their life. Later, I am informed that the doctors cannot deduce which protein, from which nut, I am allergic to. Thus, all nuts are taboo/verboten/forbidden. I am crushed.

It is a year since Sharon died, and Naomi, Eunice and I ponder what to do to mark the anniversary. Maybe a seance is in order in the appropriately named bar, The Spiritualist? Should we see the latest Bond film *No Time to Die*? In the end, we decide unanimously that a shopping spree would encapsulate the spirit of our dear one. Especially if it were very expensive and frivolous. We rise to the challenge and channel her retail energy, finishing with cocktails in a bar called Fly South in Lyndoch Street in Glasgow. Lyndoch Street in Greenock was where Sharon and her sisters were brought up by her abstemious Pentecostal parents in a flat above an off-licence. It seems particularly appropriate. It is truly a fitting homage. 'Darlinks, how wunderbar!' she would have said, approvingly. 'Loving the libations!' It was a splendid day out.

***

The mice have eaten through all your packets of Cock soup, writes Linda from France, adding the photos of shredded soup packets. *Droppings everywhere.* Yvonne had given out plentiful supplies of Cock soup that she had sourced in the Chinese supermarkets. These were regulars for inclusion in Christmas stockings.

Don't worry, I reassure Linda, *we will soon be out to serve them their eviction notice.*

It's difficult to believe that we are on a plane again. The last time was nearly two years ago. So much has changed; we have our Covid tests lined up, our *pass sanitaire* on our mobiles, our passenger locator forms downloaded and our masks on. We are going out to France for only a week, during the October school break. I remind Gerry of a Ryanair flight I took twenty years ago. Whilst in the toilet, I noticed, to my horror, that I was peeing on someone's passport; it must have inadvertently slipped out of their back pocket. I carefully fished the sodden document out of the bowl and tried to pat it dry with towels. 'Umm,' I said to a steward, in a sheepish voice, 'I found this passport in the toilet bowl, and I am really sorry, but I couldn't stop myself,' – I felt my face redden up – 'I'm afraid I have peed on it.'

With admirable insouciance, the steward grabbed the passport with a paper napkin, checked the name and waving it in the air, bellowed, 'Anyone with the name of Philomena something-or-other here? Here you are, love,' dropping it into the lap of the woman behind me. Such innocent times.

Bordeaux has had a radical makeover in the intervening years, but some things remain the same: the ubiquitous General de Gaulle Boulevard and Place des Martyrs de la Résistance. However, it specialises in quirky names for bars such as the Inglorious Bar-Star and the Café le Toulousain.

And *scorchio* it is; every morning the sun bursts forth, an enormous yellow splash. It is as if the sun is mocking Gerry with its warmth and light, because Gerry is stuck in the barn for the week. He is determined to finish up all the major jobs such as electrics and water installation for his kitchen pièce de résistance. Consequently, his complexion remains *peely-wally* and rarely does he allow himself outside to bathe in the light. Occasionally, my services are called on, to pull through wires and cables, prune wisteria, roses and vines. Generally, it is a time for me to frolic with friends, dip into pools (just warm enough) and catch up with administration and gossip: two opposing sides of pleasure. Keeping the holiday spirit afloat, I manage to read a book, *All Passion Spent* by Vita Sackville-West. The title belies the lack of lust and a penchant for semicolons, as befits a book written between the wars. However, the book title did have the effect of raising an eyebrow or two in public.

The hunters have popped up, guns cocked, ready to kill the fleeing deer in the neighbouring fields. For the second time, a wild boar runs in front of the car.

Anthea, our neighbour, is back in hospital and still recovering her speech after a stroke. She is glad that I have come to visit. 'Did you come a short camel ride away? Blummox?' She shakes her head as the words come, hesitantly, in the wrong order. Her frustration is apparent. She slowly rearranges them in a different pattern, then sinks back into the pillow, exhausted. There is a word describing a sudden breaking-off of thought: *aposiopesis.* I am just as bad; words have a tendency to rush through my brain and escape before I capture them. Something to do with my advancing years, I suspect. I agree with Anthea. Blummox!

Our friend Simon and his mate Hugh are still busy building the terrace at the back of the house. I anxiously eye the needle of the bank account, as it hovers over zero. This might be a reason why, when persuaded by Nicola and Robert to indulge in one of our favourite pastimes and visit the *vide greniers* in Villeréal and Monpazier, I buy absolutely nothing, much to the amazement of my *compagnons.* This uncharacteristic restraint, I suspect, has more to do with having spent the last two months divesting myself of furniture and belongings in order to sell the Glasgow house. I am sloughing off stuff – momentarily. Shake, shake, shake.

We are rather shocked to find that the electricity has been powered down. Possibly because the bill does not seem to be paid by direct debit anymore. Yet another puzzle to be sorted, as there are now eight houses called the same name, and it is unclear who is the culprit.

We arrange the removal of the ugly trees at the entrance to the drive to be replaced by the long pencil shapes of cypresses. At last, we have arranged for an area to be flattened in front of the house. Coutal Haut is built into a slope and we would forever sit on chairs that would keel over onto tables. The contractors duly arrive. They dislodge branches which fall and break the windows of the caravan at the side of the well, opposite the house. For good measure, they also break the telephone cable. One job down, two more created.

Irena phones with good news – she and Ant are getting married! If the wedding plans of Ziggy and Joanna are anything to go by, the event may be a long time coming. They too, plan to move to Sydney as soon as Covid restrictions are lifted. Irena recounts the *proposal* and describes the ring, which has also travelled a terrific distance. Ant's father originally comes from a Hungarian Jewish family. The ring has been in his family for generations, and he promised his beloved Hungarian grandmother that he would put it on the finger of the woman he intended to marry. The ring survived the travails of World War Two in Budapest and emigrated with the family to Australia. When Ant decided to propose to Irena, he made arrangements for the ring to be transported over to London. He didn't trust the ring to be sent by post and so the ring passed from one friend to the next, as Covid restrictions thwarted progress. Eventually, after one and a half years of travelling, the ring was safe in Ant's sweaty mitts. He took Irena by surprise by producing it during a hiking break in the Peak District. Romance still lives!

Now we are back to long queues and passport stamps in Bordeaux airport. It is a place of bedlam: people packed together (forget the one-metre distance rule), long queues (because the face scanning technology no longer works and people wear masks) and forms with necessary reference numbers that will not download. The airport employee shrugs when people come to complain. '*Oui, c'est un bordel, et alors?*' At the last minute, Gerry and I manage to navigate the damn form and run to the plane. The couple behind us jump up and down with frustration. I have never seen anyone jump like that before. They are left behind in sunny France. They would be doing double somersaults if they knew that there are Brexiteers who have blithely obtained *Cartes de Séjour* (residence permits), although they only have holiday homes in France. If the Covid restrictions don't get you, being out of Europe will.

Gerry has the last laugh. I have been the consummate European, travelling on my Polish passport, as he is subjected to passport stamps and questions. On our return to Edinburgh, the passport official says slowly to me: 'How... long... do... you... intend... staying... in... the... UK?'

'Well, I've got work next week,' I reply. My accent is definitely Scottish.

He continues, carefully enunciating his words. 'And... have... you... thought... about... settled... status?' I stare at him and whip out my trusty Saltire senior citizen bus pass, rarely used for buses but handy for international travel. (I'm still shocked that I'm eligible for it.) 'Well, why didn't you say so at the start? Away, with you!' he guffaws.

My bus pass will get me anywhere.

November & December 2021 *Twilight*

COP26 climate change summit in Glasgow is the last best hope for the world to get its act together.

John Kerry

According to John Kerry, America's climate envoy, we should heed scientists' warnings that there are only nine years remaining within which to make the most critical decisions. Boris Johnson tries at a press conference to alleviate any dip into pessimism in his opening remarks: 'The clock on the doomsday device is still ticking, but we have a bomb disposal team on site, and they are starting to snip some of the wires.'

Gas and oil are still not mentioned! The figures are stark: after forty years of warnings, thirty years of negotiations, the situation is worse. Emissions have risen by fifty per cent since

1990 and the UN predict they will rise another twenty-six per cent by 2030.

Joe Biden, Barack Obama, Boris Johnson, Emmanuel Macron and all the acolytes roll into town. Around four hundred private jets and a motorcade of gas-guzzling cars converge on Glasgow for the Climate Change Conference COP26. Joe Biden, alone, has a string of thirty-eight cars and an ambulance thrown into his convoy for good measure. Prestwick Airport, in nearby Ayrshire, is used as a jet car park, after dropping off the clientele minutes away in Glasgow Airport. After the first day, Prince Charles and Boris Johnson head back for a night in London on two different private jets. They don't even do *co-voiturage* – or should that be *co-avionage*? Whatever jet-sharing translates as. Police have been deployed in Glasgow from all around the UK. The football stadia are studded with police vans. The media have descended. One American TV crew has pitched up at Edinburgh Castle saying that it is a better backdrop to report from than Glasgow. It doesn't seem to matter where the action is.

The Greenpeace vessel, the *Rainbow Warrior*, has sailed up the Clyde with a posse of porpoises, for the perfect photo shoot. At the start of the conference, in the river, an Extinction Rebellion activist dressed up as Boris Johnson burns a boat that displays the banner, "Our children's future". Meanwhile, other activists burn stacks of fake money.

So many hopes rest on this COP. In spite of that, there is a palpable sense of distrust. The end result is what Alex Ferguson (the abrasive football manager) used to call "the squeaky-bum moment" when all the tough negotiations have to take place. In other words, squirming under pressure. This is the first COP that has mentioned fossil fuels and coal, with coal being the most polluting. Nevertheless, at the eleventh hour, following a push from India and China, the language switches from "phase out" of coal, to "phase down", prompting tears from the COP president and angry responses from European and affected countries.

After all the promises from every one of the previous twenty-five COPs, the world is still heating up towards the tipping point of 1.5 degrees. In spite of all the flowery speeches, the inevitable horse-trading alliances between countries and big business still take place. There are five hundred delegates present from companies allied with fossil fuels. It is assumed that their voices will be heard loud and clear, especially in terms of transition (buying more time) and offsetting (some other unfortunate, poorer country is landed with your rubbish). More than ever before, intersectionality is at the forefront of discussion, our changing world impacts in so many different areas. All clamour for justice. Surely, we must all agree that we cannot keep on living in the way we do.

Glasgow Cleansing Department goes on strike to coincide with the world's eyes on the city. Instead of decrying the overflowing bins, maybe it would have been a better idea to address improving working conditions for the cleansing workers. After all, the initial clap for the NHS carers did not translate into better wages for the carers, after the height of pandemic anxiety.

Let's face it, our principled stance is somewhat tinged by greed and opportunism. Our brief dispensation can surely be redeemed by atonement at some later stage. Suddenly, Glaswegians have opened their doors to thousands of visitors for a tidy sum. When a colleague mentions that she is housing an activist for free, I mumble, 'What a selfless gesture.' When pressed, I have to admit that we have rented out our house to BBC film crews for the duration of the conference. I hear her tongue click a noise of disapproval. There is no point arguing that we did not expect this to happen. Our house sold within a week, earlier in the month, and the flat we are moving into became available earlier than anticipated. A mutual friend had suggested the let. It was not something we had actively pursued… our excuses are endless. But it is manna from heaven, or rather money to pay for the work done on the terrace in Coutal Haut. We are mere conduits.

For the first week of the let, we move into our fellow Schemie Fran's house, two doors down, before trundling our suitcase down the road to the flat. It also looks over the canal, so our swans are in full view. It is like being a student again. Gerry and I have two mugs, one saucepan and a borrowed airbed that deflates in the middle of the night. We have all reverted to adolescents, giggling manically at silly jokes. 'Hey,' asks Fran, 'have you heard of the love darts of snails?'

'Love darts? What are you twittering on about? Lovebirds you mean, surely?'

Fran explains. A few years ago, she took pupils on a trip to Normandy where they visited a snail farm, as you do. It was fascinating. Fran described the box of "love darts" they were shown. The life span of a snail is only about sixty days so, ironically, they have to procreate as fast as possible, the opposite of snail's pace. Many snails are also hermaphrodites, and so the snail that shoots and places the dart with the sperm, boosting secretions into another snail whilst mating, can fertilise the other's eggs. The love darts are an essential tool for promiscuous snails, which mate multiple times with different partners to try and fertilise as many snails as they can. The snail who hits the other snail is a love rat, as the dart carries a gene that reduces the fertility and life span of the receiver. Winner takes all; who would have thought that snails could be so sneaky? So un-Cupid? And why would they want to harm the mother of his/her genes? It's thought that reducing the chances of the mother procreating again boosts the lineage of the snail darter. I was reminded by my Aunt Yvonne that I used to look after her snails when she went off on holiday, and she had told me all about love darts. The knowledge must have been secreted in my brain all this time.

The BBC asks us to do a few linen changeovers and at this point we get a chance to whip out from the house some necessities such as socks, walking boots, frying pan and my beloved hot water bottle. 'Ah, we forgot a wooden spoon,' I say, knocking my head with my fist. I note, with disappointment, that the packet of Tunnock's teacakes we had provided as a welcome gift lies unopened on the kitchen table. Some things are unfathomable. Still, success can be measured by being able to wash and by wearing clean clothes every day. There is no point in filling up the new flat with our things, as we will have to clear it soon enough in order to sand and polish the walnut floors. The planks squeak when we walk on them, "nightingale floors", they call them in Japan, all the better to hear intruders coming in the middle of the night. The novelty wears thin after a few nights. The cacophony of the songbirds is getting on our nerves. I now understand the popularity of the Japanese "fortune houses", or glorified sheds, stuffed to the gunnels with people's possessions whilst Japanese homes are famously airy and sparsely furnished. How liberating to be unencumbered by possessions. For a short while at least.

A bout of ill-health dissuades the Queen from coming to Glasgow. For a brief, petrifying second, the possibility of the demise of the Queen at this particular moment looks as if it may precipitate the end of talks. What would happen then? Luckily, the sprightly ninety-five-year-old David Attenborough is in attendance and his dignified presence and wise words dwarf the inadequacies of the slumping Joe Biden and Boris Johnson. The latter sitting beside the anthropologist with his eyes closed and not wearing a mask. The smell of corruption lingers when the prime minister decides to change parliamentary rules on lobbying to defend a fellow politician for speaking on behalf of companies who paid him for the service. Ah, one yearns for the good old days, when, allegedly, politicians received brown envelopes stuffed with cash! It's therefore refreshing when Leonardo DiCaprio flies in on a commercial flight and attends an event for COP26 round the corner from us, in Maryhill. Greta Thunberg is not exactly glugging down the Buckfast. She is filmed in Pollok singing, *You can shove your climate change up your arse*, to the tune of the local folk song, "Ye Canny Shove Yer Grannie Aff a Bus", albeit with a posh burr. She'll soon be *wee Greta fae Glasgae gie'n it laldy*.

I join a friend, Briony, and her daughter, in the Friday climate change march from Kelvingrove Park to George Square. We find ourselves marching behind some of my pupils. They look aghast when they spot me, given that I had berated one of them the day before on the lack of action on the homework front. There are some novel banners on show, apart from the more obvious ones calling for action. One activist holds up one saying, "Don't talk to blue bib cops – they're here to gather intelligence on you and other protestors" and hovers beside some irritated-looking police with blue bibs on. Another banner held aloft by some veiled young women, says "Eat pussy not animals #GoVegan". Yet another banner proclaims the laudable wish, "Think for yourself, act for others". The radio presenter announced in the morning that there would be a carnival atmosphere, but the police sectioned up the walk of twenty-five thousand people, mainly schoolchildren, women and toddlers. Therefore, it took far longer than anticipated to walk to the city centre. I do not know if this was a safety issue, but for the more vulnerable it was too long to wait. They left when the demonstration neared the square. The train station toilets are closed and the speeches last one and a half hours. People listen patiently, as a helicopter circles overhead, nearly drowning out the speakers. It is almost dark when wee Greta appears and electrifies the crowd with her presence. People power! I look down to see an empty Coca-Cola can on the ground. I bend down, pop it in my rucksack and head home.

The next day brings the main event, the big march against climate change. I mutter under my breath to Gerry, 'Wish this climate would change, demonstrating in Glasgow is rain, more rain and endless rain.' If I thought that yesterday there was too much hanging around, then organising 150,000 people is an even bigger challenge. Not helped by presumably bored police, overreacting to a peaceful demonstration and kettling a few protestors. For much of the time, we march with the delegates of Pacific nations, whose countries are suffering the full wrath of climate change. Despite the cold and the fact that they are scantily clad, they are nevertheless in good spirits. I recount a tale of a colleague who grew up in Santa Lucia. His mother once caught him with his head in the fridge and she asked him what he was doing.

'Just trying to find out what it's like to live in a cold country,' he mumbled. I secretly thought that he had his chops around a Battenburg cake.

It is beginning to grow dark when we reach Glasgow Green. Gerry, Fran and I wrap up our wet Palestinian flags; as Fran contemplates a warm bath, dinner and *Strictly Come Dancing* on TV, Gerry and I prepare for Part Two of our evening by chucking green paint on our faces and dressing like tramps. Our friend, Liz, is obsessed with Halloween and for the last two years has not managed to host one of her fabled parties. The party has been delayed for various reasons until early November. As we approach their lit-up cottage in Fintry,

Gerry clutching his hollowed-out turnip (I must explain, pumpkins just will not do), we can see the Halloween attic has been emptied into the house. Talking skeletons, vampires, bats, the whole ghoulish shebang prevails! Liz looks pleased and has returned to her usual antagonistic self. 'You'd better have brought your *tumshie* (turnip), Gerry, *or else!*'

I spent much of our time in France moving stones about and now, here in Glasgow, the leitmotif is moving boxes. Downsizing by a third, from a three-storey house to a tiny flat where the deck is bigger than the flat itself, is a challenge. Despite giving away furniture, clothes and household items to friends, various community groups and charities, our rented storage space in the centre of the city is now crammed full of our possessions. The boxes have been imbued with magical triffid qualities and seem to multiply. Indeed, every space in the flat is now, officially, a boxroom. Even the two tiny bedrooms, which have been well named because, indeed, there is only room for a bed in each of them. The problem is solved by dumping one of the beds so that the full glory of boxes can be exhibited. Ferrying boxes that have travelled with me from one attic to another seems to be one of my pastimes. Some boxes are marked "sort through 2015" and even one, "sort through 2013". My life in boxes is further compounded, when I am informed that a community policeman is about to take residence in the school where I work. Thereafter, I have to move from my classroom to the end of the corridor. My work life is now a frenzy of teaching, binning a career full of lovingly curated resources and, surprise, carting boxes. 'Why don't you just have a massive bonfire?' suggests Vinny, my long-suffering colleague, who has been roped in for donkey work. 'How come you have so many boxes?'

At home, there are some items that we cannot bear to

relinquish: the sleigh-bed, a giant mirror and an ancient chest of drawers, on which the patina shines through from years of usage, to name a few. They are all sent to France. As they are lifted into the van by muscular Lithuanians from the removal company, I long to sneak into the back as a stowaway. Incredibly, our precious objects reach Coutal Haut, intact, in forty-eight hours. Simon, our friend, phones. 'Everything is dumped in the barn. You'll have a lot of unpacking to do when you eventually get here!'

My Aunt Magda has died of cancer in Paris. Her wish was that she and Zygmunt, her husband, would both die at the same moment and intertwine as one tree. I wish that tree could be planted in Coutal Haut.

A recollection surfaces. Zygmunt, as well as being very religious, loves history and insisted that Magda, Gerry and I join him to watch the film *La Reine Margot* on the TV. In the late sixteenth century, France was in a political turmoil as Protestants (Huguenots) and Catholics fought for control of the country. The daughter of the scheming Catherine de Medici, Margot, was caught up in the feud and offered up in marriage to form a political alliance. Zygmunt obviously thought that the film would be a faithful, serious portrayal of historical facts. We all sat together, squashed on the sofa for an uncomfortable hour and a half, as the celebrity heartthrob of the time, Isabelle Adjani, shagged her lover at every opportunity. These opportunities seemed to be countless, up alleyways, against walls and even on beds. At the end of the film, Magda turned to a visibly shell-shocked and disapproving Zygmunt and said, 'Well, they seem to have had a lot of energy. Anyone for dessert?' All unpleasantness was put to bed after we held hands and sang hymns together, our souls partially cleansed.

The *panthenisation* is the act of honouring French citizens who have bestowed glory on *l'Héxagone* by interring their remains in the famous mausoleum, the Panthéon, in the centre of Paris. This caused a slight controversy of late. It is up to the discretion of the incumbent president to decide who is going to be thus honoured. Is it cynical to think that Macron's choice of Joséphine Baker has something to do the upcoming elections in May? After all, she ticks all boxes that will enhance his reputation: Baker was a universalist, a black civil rights activist and an American who fought in the French Resistance. It has also been discovered that her ancestors originally came from the island of Martinique in the Caribbean, which is still a French colony. Most importantly, she was a woman. Only two other women have had the honour of entering the Panthéon, and "La Baker" was a woman who chose France over America, "the land of the free". As she observed, 'I have walked into the palaces of kings and queens and into the houses of presidents, but I could not walk into a hotel in America and get a cup of coffee, and that made me mad.'

She was standing beside Martin Luther King Jr in 1968, when he made his famous "I Have a Dream" speech, wearing her Free French uniform. Intriguingly, none of her remains will actually be taken to the hallowed place of the Panthéon; it is rather a symbolic gesture. Her family insisted that her body remain in Monaco. Instead, the Panthéon coffin was filled with soil from the USA, France and Monaco.

I too feel a tad smug. Her elevated position means that more people will visit the south-west of France, where she lived with her "rainbow" family, the children she adopted from all around the world.

Incidentally, I feel a sense of pride that a Polish woman, the physicist Marie Curie, also resides in the Panthéon, albeit in a lead coffin. There were fears that her remains might be radioactive.

Only deadlines can concentrate the mind. My daughter Irena, fiancé Ant, childhood friend Amel (who spent many holidays with us in Coutal Haut) and her boyfriend come up to Glasgow for a wedding and stay in the flat. Gerry and I are back to wearing our fetching hazmat numbers to whitewash all the walls and ceiling. By accident, not design, we are the movers, decorators, builders and cleaners. Gerry builds shelves in every nook and cranny. Already, the shed on the deck is full of wood, ready for further expansion. My stepbrother, Richard, had to step down from moving duties due to a health problem. So, on the wettest weekend imaginable (and this is Glasgow), Gerry and I carry settees, tables, the full kit and caboodle along the street and chuck most of it over onto the deck. Then starts the almighty cleaning of the house. This is perhaps the best way to eradicate any residual nostalgia or sentimental attachment to bricks and mortar in the place once called home. The evening before the house sale's completion, the house shines, duly scrubbed. My passport is retrieved from the back of a radiator. We close the door and mutter with satisfaction, 'Goodbye, *you bastard*.'

The news from the outside world is bleak. Extremes of temperature, wildfires and floods ravage the land in biblical proportions. Waves and waves of migrants, desperate people, crash onto our shores in flimsy boats. Lifeless bodies float in the icy waters, flotsam and jetsam. Meanwhile, billionaires float in space, strutting their vanity and wealth by projecting themselves out of the world and, unfortunately for us, coming back to land. Ministers push forward the Nationality and Borders Bill, which undermines the 1951 Geneva Convention, stripping British citizenship from those who have somehow displeased the powers that be, then sends "home" those whose ancestors came from a foreign land. In effect, it will impact most, those people of ethnic origin. Meanwhile, the government seeks to replace the Human Rights Act with a British Bill of Rights. Thus, the UK is no longer answerable to the European Court in Strasbourg. Cats and dogs take precedence in the flights out of Afghanistan, leaving behind devastation, desperation and rusting weaponry. British tourists, unless they have a compelling reason to travel, are turned back from France. We are unclean. We are led by a string of throttlebottoms: inept people in public office. What they need is an easy war for deflection, to halt the whisperings of failures.

Israel deems six renowned Palestinian human rights organisations to be terrorists. Elsewhere, the crackdown on democracy is in full swing by the Chinese authorities in Hong Kong. All resistance to occupation and dissent is now classed as terror. From time to time, the case of Nazanin Zaghari-Ratcliffe, the British woman detained behind bars in Iran, is aired as the injustice meted out by a cruel regime. What is not mentioned is that the Iranians will release her once Britain returns the £400 million debt owed to Iran. (She is indeed released a few months later when Britain repays the debt.) So much of our world view is becoming increasingly blurred through the lens of Britannia.

Time to clamber down from my soapbox. It's just too slippy.

There is much to drive me ballistic closer to home. Self-scanning payment machines in supermarkets, people the same age as me addressing me as "dear", people not picking up their dog poo and the proposed reintroduction of the imperial measurement system of feet and inches, pounds, pints and ounces. Soon I will be paid in threepenny bits. For solace, I return to my own wee world, paddling around in the shallows. Time to hunt for the perfect potting shed on the internet.

As a distraction, I turn the radio on and listen to a clip about lighthouse work. It seems so appealing. A beacon warning against imminent disasters. A few seconds later, it dawns on me that the subject is light housework. There is nowhere to run.

Boris Johnson addresses the CBI (Confederation of British Industry), loses his notes, and nearly his sanity, when he brightly perks up: 'Ever been to Peppa Pig World?' The leaders of business look at him aghast and uncomprehendingly. Nothing can save his bacon at this stage, surely. Nevertheless, the British public will keep on voting for him, regardless of the pig's ear the country has become. He testiculates wildly, arms flailing, all swagger and bluster. Bollocks and mince keep on coming out of his mouth. No matter the fact that Christmas parties were thrown at No.10 Downing Street whilst the rest of the country was in lockdown. Nor that the hoi polloi who were found to have flouted the rules were heavily fined. No matter, that the police on duty outside 10 Downing Street can easily identify those who attended said parties, no matter that the minister charged with investigating this matter had himself had a party in his office. None of this seems to matter at all. Even if Boris was trussed up like a turkey with a boomerang shoved up his *bahookie*, whilst spouting Churchillian bon mots, the great British public would likely shake its head and keep voting into power his venal and duplicitous party.

To quote a Hollywood director, 'You think I know fuck nothing – I know fuck *all*!'

In the end, it's all pish and wind, nothing of substance.

It looks like the UK Government is about to sink in a cesspool of sleaze and corruption. After all, Macron, has apparently said that the British have voted for a circus led by a clown. Then, as Christmas nears, a miracle happens. A new variant virus is born: Omicron.

Omigod. My head slumps.

We will forever be swirling inside one virus-infested swamp or another. Then another miracle: the prime minister's wife gives birth to a baby girl, and so he is conveniently indisposed. And lo, Boris Johnson and his government have their bacon saved.

Swans emerge from the fog on the canal, two gleaming white swans. They must be the parents, but what of their offspring? A few days later, the two adults reappear with one white and brown teenager tagging along beside them. The remaining teenager is nowhere to be seen. The following day, we witness the almighty flap of wings, their ecstatic rush out of the water into the air.

After the Beast from the East and the Pest from the West, Storm Arwen arrives with a massive whoosh and devastates the north of the country. It seems like a metaphor for what is happening presently in the UK.

Sharon's sixtieth birthday would have been on 22 December. The Lancaster Rose on the deck has just, just, and no more, hung onto its last red bloom in celebration. Rocco howls at the full moon. 'This is not a shape-shifting event, of *that* I am certain,' Sharon would have said.

Gerry and I, together with my Irena and fiancé Ant, spend Christmas Eve, the "Polish Wygilia", with my mother and stepfather. On the alternative Christmas morning, we visit the wildlife rescue sanctuary where Gerry's sister Jackie volunteers. Much as I love the playful seals, I am smitten by the "street swans". These are swans who have been rescued from the tarmac, seeking better pickings. Even after a bit of rehabilitation and being rehoused on a watery landscape, some stubbornly persist in their urban dream and return to the streets. Maybe our teenage swan is to be found there. We keep an anxious lookout from our window.

A slight change of view: a man in a kilt, gliding silently down the canal on his paddle board.

Fifteen

Letter to Sharon

I'm going to kill the next person who says "have you thought about...", "don't you think it would be better...", "if I were you I would...", "a hook on the bathroom door would be helpful...", "ever thought about a mirror above the sink?" as they cast their critical eye about our house. Nothing rankles us more. As if we have spent the last four years lying in bed chomping cheese baguettes. Alternatively, I will kill the person who says to me "why don't you write about this?".

Practically nothing has been done with the garden. I know; you would have it planned, drawn and executed by now. I could blame the pandemic (it did go on so), but really the truth is I am swithering about what to plant. In an ideal world, the slope would be sliced up into Italianate terraces, each one bearing fruit, vegetables, olive trees and bright-coloured flowers. The lavender and rosemary hedge I planted two years ago has been totally obscured by tumbling brambles; the fruit trees still have not been pruned. You may have seen the terrace hewn out the back; now it is flat and concreted with tubes leading out of the walls; these will be future lights. At the back, there is even all the necessary equipment for a swimming pool, should one of the children raise the cash to install one. I fear it won't be in my lifetime. Still, one can dream. We don't have the travertine tiles laid on the terrace yet. You raved about them, but *festina lente*, it will happen soon. Especially as I am now ensconced here alone most of the time with Rocco.

Gerry and I only had three weeks to get everything ready for your interment.

Interment? It sounds so grand.

Not as grand as you might think, but you would have enjoyed the banter, the laughter, the food and drink. A *fête de l'amitié*, a true celebration of your life.

We all looked our best; I had visited the hairdresser that morning and overheard the gossip. There was a general consensus that the *circulation*, the traffic, has become intolerable in the brimming metropolis that is Villeréal.

Who cares about your barnet or the circulation? What about my interment?

You were simply tipped out and mixed with the earth under an Albizia tree on your favourite spot beside the sunflowers, overlooking the valley. The precise place that you used to meditate on all the things you would do in the future. Better to be on top looking down. I'm sure you'd agree. A sunny spot, no dreich Glasgow weather for you. The silhouetted boxing hares which you ordered for my birthday present, and which arrived posthumously, are now placed at your side. They stand poised, ready to take on any moles, *loirs* or other beasties who trespass on your gaff. Your false eyelashes have fared well in the heat; they make the hares' eyes come alive. Eunice and Naomi threatened to chuck in some banana skins, Brussel sprouts, dried tomatoes and avocados beside you, as payback for leaving them with such a massive bureaucratic nightmare to sort out. Your ceremony was simple and solemn; tears were shed. Only twelve people present. More would have been invited, but the post-Covid travel chaos has still not abated. The prospect of wailing, stranded people to round up and sort out was too much for me to contemplate. Of course, you had the last word: we played the rendition of "Ae Fond Kiss" that you had sung for our Burns Supper three years ago.

Every morning I am out watering the Albizia tree.

Darlink, water is not my favourite beverage, as you are very well aware. Just saying...

Things would have been so much easier if we had been able to come over at Easter. Many of our belongings had been transported over from Glasgow by the muscular Lithuanian removal contractors in December and March. The wee flat can only accommodate wee things, hence, instead of a sofa, we had two deckchairs in the living room for six months. I have inherited your comfy sheepskin slippers with S emblazoned on one and L on the other.

You're welcome.

Linda and Ian were on hand to instruct them where to dump the big piles of boxes and furniture, which further enhanced the look of the builder's yard. All the more to deter burglars.

We had already booked our flights to France when we got the call from Ziggy to say that he and Joanna were going to get married in Sydney, at long last. No way would I miss my son's wedding. So, it was back to the drawing board and more flight tickets consigned to the bin.

You know how we had booked the flights and hotel for Ziggy's big, fat Polish wedding on 6 June 2020? You had already decided on the dress you would wear, booked the Irena Eris Spa at the hotel and, despite being ill at the time, were determined to get match fit.

'Białystok, here I come!' you said. But, in the end, no one could go; Covid restrictions put a stop to that.

'You must be desperate to get married,' I said to Ziggy. He and Joanna had to ward off bush fires, drought, pestilence, floods and war before eventually tying the knot on a beautiful promontory overlooking a beach near Terrigal in New South Wales.

War? I hear you say.

Haud yer wheesht. I'll get round to that. There is so much you have missed.

The Australian lockdown had been draconian. Even Australians had not been allowed to fly back home in the last two years. So, as soon as restrictions were lifted, there was a clamour for flight tickets. *No way will I miss my son's wedding,* I thought again grimly. However, definitely not as resolutely as before, as I handed over about £5k for our tickets. Mind you, the family in front of us in the queue when we were waiting to board had obviously bought tickets before the pandemic. The mother was complaining so that all could hear, that having paid £36k for first-class tickets, she expected a better sort of service.

After a few days recuperating at my Uncle Ted's motel in Sydney, we made our way to Terrigal. Ziggy had played football for Central Coast Mariners and was now playing for Western Sydney Wanderers. However, both he and Joanna loved living in a chilled seaside resort in a rented flat overlooking the Pacific. Ziggy had chosen to drive the three hours round trip to his club throughout the week with the occasional night over at Ted's. Typical of Ziggy, he told us that he had arranged a flat for Gerry, me, his dad, David and his girlfriend, Jane. What he had failed to mention was, although it had a decent bedroom, living/kitchen with bathroom (which in a fit of generosity we offered to David and Jane), the downstairs was something that Fritzl would have approved of.

Ah, Fritzl. I approve.

I remember you were always fascinated by the story of Fritzl. (Fritzl was the Austrian monster who had kept his daughter imprisoned in the basement of his home. It was a cause célèbre in 2008. After twenty-four years, his daughter, who had borne him seven children in captivity, eventually managed to escape her life of abuse and degradation.) What everyone wanted to know was what was Mrs Fritzl doing up the stairs whilst eight of her family were down in the basement? Surely, she must have heard something? What did she think of her husband's massive shopping haul every week? Anyway, in truth, our basement was not that bad. Two bunkbeds on either side of the room, a strip of fluorescent lighting, iron bars and shades on the window. No sun for us. We envied Joanna's parents luxuriating in the penthouse suite with Ziggy and Joanna overlooking the ocean.

Perhaps that's not fair. The latest wedding was supposed to have taken place on 2 July in the original venue, just outside Białystok. In the event, the war was progressing steadily towards the border and four million refugees were flooding into Poland. Therefore, it was decided that it would be best to cancel and have a scaled-down affair in Australia. Unless, of course, as I mischievously muttered, it would be a good way of cutting down on unwanted guests.

BUT WHAT WAR? WHO IS AT WAR?

Oh, I know you must be exasperated by now, Sharon.

Shush – coming to that.

You would have loved Ziggy and Joanna's wedding. It was on a gloriously sunny day and the Scots were sweating in their kilts. 'Where are we?' I asked.

'Where I belong,' answered a fellow guest.

'Yes,' I persisted, 'but it's not where I belong. Go on, give me a clue.'

'Where I belong,' he repeated. I looked at the invitation in my hand. There it was: Wyrrabalong Lookout, Cromarty Hill Rd, Bateau Bay. Aboriginal land. They had found a Scottish minister from the Uniting Church in Australia (what is that?) with a thick Dundonian accent despite his forty years in the country. He made constant football allusions during his spiel, "ooh we have an equaliser! Ziggy has just scored himself a wife!". All these things you would have loved. And did you know that Mary Wollstonecraft Shelley wrote *Frankenstein* in Dundee?

How will I ever know if you knew that?

Only nine relatives managed to come over from Europe. The remainder of the party was formed by Uncle Ted, his partner Nita and Ziggy's new Ozzie friends. By a stroke of sheer luck, Irena and Ant were present at the wedding as well. They are preparing to move out to Sydney at the end of the year. It gave us an opportunity to meet the other in-laws, and we spent a pleasant afternoon lunching with them at their home in Sydney and feeding the kookaburras in the old gum trees in their garden. Irena and Ant are hell-bent on selling their flat in London. Apparently, Sydney is one of the most expensive places to buy property now. Gerry was astonished at the prices of his previous abode in Neutral Bay. It was at least thirty-five years ago, I remind him. Think of what Ruchill was like at that time: decayed, forgotten. I can't remember which part in Sydney you lived in, Sharon. Yes, I know it was for five years, and you had a swimming pool, and it was luxurious, but I couldn't come and visit because I had two toddlers in tow.

Hmm. I have a feeling that you are missing out some vital gossip here.

Get out of my ear, Sharon.

This time, being free of impediments, Gerry and I managed to spend a couple of days sightseeing, walking around the city with his friend John, from his shipyard days, accompanied by his wife, Lesley. We walked around Circular Quay, Woolloomooloo, Surry Hills, Harbour Rocks and Darling Harbour soaking up the atmosphere.

I had been keen to view the exhibition of maps in the State Library. The library is one of the few old-fashioned ones left that smells of wax polish and is lined with thousands of books around the walls with a central part full of tables and chairs. It was just like the Mitchell Library in Glasgow used to be. Interesting though the exhibition was, the photos of Aboriginal women in the outback, taken in the latter part of the nineteenth century, showing them completely constrained in whalebone corsets, Victorian clothes and wide hats, was even more so. What caught my eye even more, was the exhibit on female convicts, brought from Britain, to serve out their sentences in Van Diemen's Land (Tasmania today), between 1844–1852. From a total of around twenty-four thousand women transported to Australia, 12,500 found themselves in Tasmania. The government records on display give an idea of the cruelty of the system. Most of the women were working-class and first-time offenders. One mother of three, called Maria Birkinshall, from York, was sentenced to seven years for stealing a shawl in mid-winter. I wonder if she ever got back to England, or if she ever saw her own children again. All these tragic stories and they were not so long ago, in terms of generations. After all, my own grandfather (my father's father) had been born in 1886.

The Anzac Memorial was intriguing, built to honour the Australian dead. They had gone to fight in other people's wars. One plaque said, "Memorial extension was opened by a grandson of the Queen, 20 October 2018". We wondered if that was the grandson who should not be mentioned by name. Then on another Anzac memorial, "A soldier set this stone 19 July 1922". One of the people who worked there explained that no names were mentioned, to indicate that every soldier who died was equal in death. Instead, the places where they came from festooned the walls in alphabetical order. I wrote down my favourites: Come by Chance, (there is a place with the same name in Newfoundland), Como, Goonoo Goonoo, Gordon (for obvious reasons) German Creek now Empire Vale Creek (also for obvious reasons, but maybe it will change again in the future), Nevernever, Nevertire. The names of the battles and campaigns in which these young soldiers fought covered the walls: Egypt, Palestine, Romani, Gaza, Beersheba, Jordan Valley, Damascus, to name but a few.

The Vietnam War in the 1960s polarised the Australian public into questioning their participation in foreign wars. Some saw the fighting as necessary to oppose the expansion of Communism in Asia. Others questioned the need for the war, the way it was fought and the reintroduction of conscription. Partisan media coverage fuelled the conflict, and protests often became violent. It was a defining event for a whole generation.

Oh my God, would you stop wittering on? TELL ME ABOUT THE WAR!

I hear you, Sharon. Just doing a spot of meandering. Anyway, it's an apposite juncture to discuss the war.

Russia invaded Ukraine in February 2022. Without going into the whys and wherefores, suffice to say that Russia is now a pariah as far as EU states and the USA are concerned. The boycott against Russia has affected stability in Europe and the import of gas and food, such as wheat. Wasn't Ukraine once described as the breadbasket of the West? No more chicken kievs in the supermarket. It's chicken kyiv now and Russian fudge has been removed from the shelves. The response in the West to take in Ukrainian refugees has been overwhelming; even Lot-et-Garonne has sheltered some Ukrainian families. People are raising money everywhere – in schools, in the streets – for the Ukrainian cause. Ziggy and Joanna had a Ukrainian flag draped over their veranda in Terrigal. I taught Ukrainian children in school in Glasgow. Gerry and I even attended an art show in Glasgow at the end of June in aid of Ukraine, whereby at least one hundred well-known artists had donated their work. The helpers were smartly turned out in yellow and blue T-shirts, and the good and the great were there, buying art and tucking into the canapés.

This is how it should be; everyone should strive to help those innocent victims of war, people caught in the crossfire. Yet, there is a growing distrust, as to the motives of politicians on either side, with any questioning of the media criticised. To hark back to the Australian participation in the Vietnam War, "Partisan media coverage fuelled the conflict". It jars with "other" refugees being shunted to Rwanda, the legacy of the Windrush generation, Dunure Street and countless other difficulties and racism they face. No outstretched arms to welcome them.

I know where this is going, hen. It's going to Palestine, isn't it?

You know me too well, Sharon.

It's too late to thank you for your support, doing turns at our fundraisers, coming with us to Palestine. I remember you chatting to the children in Aida refugee camp in Bethlehem, visiting Christ's birthplace in the Church of the Holy Sepulchre. 'Fair tarted up,' you said. The headteacher

189

in Glasgow at the school I worked in commented on my "interest in the Middle East". Jesus wept. The country/land that cannot be mentioned.

There was the usual bombing of Gaza earlier in the year. Again, barely mentioned in the press. At least there was some coverage of the killing of the Palestinian journalist, Shireen Abu Akleh by an Israeli sniper in May 2022. Both and Gerry and I gave public speeches. Here is a snippet of mine:

...our constant lament over the years is the silence of politicians, as well as the media, noticeably the BBC, in the face of the Israeli occupation, the destruction of Palestine, the theft of land and resources. If the death of Shireen has any meaning, then maybe it is to speak openly about Palestine. Maybe cracks are appearing in the wall of silence. In many places, such as Berlin, commemorations about the Nakba are banned. Germany banned the planned vigil by a pro-Palestinian Jewish group in memory of Shireen. The German police said that it falls under the ban of protests in the run-up to Nakba Day. So many people still don't understand what the Nakba means. In 1948, 750,000 Palestinians, three-quarters of the population, were killed, or made to live out the rest of their lives as refugees.

Today, Palestinians continue to be moving targets as the West remains, in the main, unmoved. The BBC will not change its stance, as it is clear that the organisation is the mouthpiece of the government, who are a leading trading partner with Israel, helpfully supplying them with arms to disarm themselves of the Palestinian "problem". And now, with the appalling situation in Ukraine, we can see clearly the hypocrisy of the stance of the West and the USA. Immediately, the DEC, the Disaster Emergency Committee, galvanised action to raise funds to help Ukraine. You will have heard all the soundbites by now about the victims of Ukraine. The BBC refused to put out an appeal to help Palestinians when Israel bombarded Gaza in 2014. Similarly, in 2009, Tony Benn rebuked the BBC (on the BBC itself!) for refusing to put out a DEC appeal for an earlier bombardment of Gaza. The BBC presenter lamely suggested that any aid sent would surely be used by Hamas for nefarious purposes. Benn angrily stated that the BBC follows orders from the Israeli Embassy in order to put the lid on any criticism of Israel.

Did you notice any of our politicians displaying Palestinian flags on their jacket lapels as they do in support of Ukraine? Indeed, flicking through the newspapers, I noted the huge number of fundraising activities for the Ukraine. When I went to my local supermarket, I was asked to add a donation for Ukraine onto the bill when I was paying for my groceries. The same happened when I called into the bookshop next door.

You will have heard all the soundbites now: the passionate rhetoric about the illegality of occupations, occupied people's right to armed resistance and that it should not be considered terrorism. The importance of sovereignty and national autonomy are loudly emphasised. What do you know? All this time, and no one told us! We were told that sanctions don't work, that we must be impartial and tell both sides of the story. As well as our friends in Palestine, we had better let our friends in Iraq, Libya, Yemen, Afghanistan and Kashmir know about this. Then we remember: justice

is for some, not for others. Here in Britain, as refugees
are pointed in the direction of Rwanda and chided for
coming over in leaky boats, other refugees are welcomed
with open arms. There have been some moments of dark
humour: Nancy Pelosi reading out Bono's yucky poem
in the US senate, the Israelis touted as negotiators for
peace, cancelling a football match with Russia as a show
of solidarity with Ukraine, chosen Ukrainians sent over
to settle on stolen Palestinian land. The huge wad of
racist politicians crying crocodile tears.

All of us who fight for Palestinian human rights
constantly fight against being silenced. We have to
fight against being labelled anti-Semitic when we call
out for justice for the Palestinians. The conflation of
criticism of Israel with anti-Semitism is ubiquitous.
Everyone should be aware of universal human rights
and the UN convention for the rights of the child, the
occupation of Palestine condemned by international
law, how apartheid operates in Israel/Palestine, how
there are five different types of permits given to the
population which determine how good your life is
going to be. If we can speak openly about Ukraine,
then we must speak about Palestine. We too should
wear our badges with pride and hope that one day our
voices will also be heard.

Sharon, are you listening? After all, you did ask! All wars
have the same basic ingredients. Domination of one side
over another. I have a sneaking admiration for Palestine
Action and Extinction Rebellion and all those who go out
and strike on our behalf. What are we going to do; what's the
alternative?

Ask nicely for change?

Yes, and I understand. I think you are going off on a tangent, though. Enough of your pontification. Is this summer in Aquitaine? What have I been missing?

The usual shenanigans! Let us start then, summer in Aquitaine, 2022.

Sixteen

Aquitaine, Summer, 2022, *Sunlight*

Travel chaos was well in place at the start of the summer, with restricted bus and train services. The evening before we were due to leave, we were informed that our flights were cancelled. We threw money at another flight, took a taxi from airport to airport and somehow arrived home in Coutal Haut. On arrival, we discovered that the well cover was about to fall into the well and there was no internet, telephone or French TV. This was compounded by our bank card being snaffled up by the cash dispenser. This meant we had to visit the bank frequently to ask for a wad of cash. Six weeks later, despite stalking the SFR (mobile phone) shop in Villeneuve and knowing every one of the employees by name, there was still no internet or phone. Thankfully, between the SFR engineer and France Telecom, the problems were fixed, just in time for Sharon's interment at the end of July.

There was a small matter of a lack of accommodation. We had not managed to finish (or start) one of the barn bedrooms, due to the earlier trip to Australia. Gerry donned his cyberware, weathered the searing heat and laboured night and day for three weeks. Lo, a bedroom emerged a day before *les visiteurs* arrived. The room looked like a monk's cell with white stone walls, a concrete floor and all set off by a hanging tapestry I had bought in a local *vide grenier* five years previously. This had previously been hoofed back to Scotland then returned in the aforementioned packing cases. As Gerry toiled in the bedroom, I dismantled the mountain of belongings congregating in the heart of our home. Surprisingly, there was a space for everything and only a few items were deemed redundant. A swan had emerged!

Linda had kindly swept cobwebs, cleaned the kitchen and our bedroom before we arrived. She had also put down sachets of mouse poison. The mice had scarpered before we reached Coutal, although I was obliged to thoroughly wash the Big Slipper (the much-loved foot muff used extensively in winter) which had temporarily accommodated a nesting mouse family. I wondered why I had adopted a lopsided gait until I realised that they had guzzled half of the rubber from the soles of my sandals. We now know categorically that mice love polystyrene. They ate and piddled on the big polystyrene sheets destined for ceiling insulation. We also know that they categorically hate the wire wool variety of insulation, because that was left untouched. Handy for us, as now wire wool insulation is under the rooftiles. Their biggest crime, however, was locating the few precious Coutal soaps we had made a few years back. All packed with argan powder, lemon and thyme. The *sleekit* mice didn't even consume the whole lot; instead, they had artfully nibbled bits and pieces from each bar. Gerry installed a *garde-manger*, a food safe on the wall, so we would see how they navigated that.

My friend Aileen told me, that after returning to her student flat after the summer, she discovered that her wooden cooking spoons had a somewhat scraggy edge. The remnants of food must have been evident to hungry mice, who also ate the crotches of knickers left soaking in a bucket underneath the sink. *Miam miam.* How tasty.

It could be worse. Bats seem to be the eternal problem around here, although no one mentions them, lest they get into trouble with the authorities. One friend (she pleads for anonymity) loves to see the little bats (pipistrelles) fly around the living room at night but was less than pleased to find that some had taken a liking to the flypapers impregnated with all bat-delicious and fly-delicious yumminess. After having partaken of a licking session, they were found dead on the kitchen floor in the morning. I reasoned that theirs was the ultimate happy death. They were destined for bat heaven. I regarded bats with a new-found respect when I discovered that they can eat one thousand mosquitos in an hour. However, recently, my friend was horrified to find big bats of the Dracula variety, roosting behind the shutters of her *salon*. Maybe just housing a humble mouse family in Coutal Haut is not the scourge I imagined it to be.

Unfortunately, the beautiful carpet in our living room succumbed to the moisture from the floor (the quarry tiles are laid directly on the earth) and disintegrated underfoot. When other carpets were unrolled, moths flew out, having chomped through big chunks, and so they too were destined for the *déchetterie*.

Linda and Ian had kept a beady eye on the property for us over the last year. There had been a spate of break-ins, as burglars took advantage of those who were absent because of Covid. Ron and Janet, long-term neighbours, had been especially disgruntled by some opportunistic thieves who had run off with a child's paddling pool (still in the box), their ancient TV, a casserole dish and the key fob to the bins and *déchetterie*. Key fobs are like gold dust, and we were all astounded to discover that the thief had actually used it *a number of times*. (Most likely, it had been sold on for an exorbitant amount.)

There has also been a spate of deaths. On the same day that Jill and Simon's son got married in a local château, and Ziggy and Joanna were supposed to be married in Białystok, we found ourselves joining a few others at Anthea's wake. Bill (her husband) made sure that the wine was plentiful, the Iberico ham on the rack was carefully sliced into slivers, and we toasted the beautiful, dignified lady that was Anthea. As Gerry and I were minding Jill and Simon's dogs at the time, I was continually racing up and down the road to check on them. The night before, they made the Jack Russell Big Escape, as they caught the whiff of something rather exciting and belted over the sunflower fields. An hour later, darkness began to descend, and we went out hunting for them in earnest, Gerry in the car and me on foot. Eventually, with relief, we rounded up the wee buggers. We didn't know how we were going to break the news to Jill and Simon had we lost their dogs.

Anthea had bookmarked her favourite sayings in David Cecil's book, Library Looking Glass: A Personal Anthology:

> *If you believe in a God, follow him*
> *If you do not believe in a God – be God-like.*

Marcus Aurelius

But I preferred this one written by a man on the death of his mother-in-law:

Cremate, bury or embalm
Take no chances!

Somewhat reminiscent of Gerry's take on the same sentiment:

We didn't know whether to cremate her or bury her
Then we thought: why not just let her live?

Véronique, Anthea's friend, explained why there was a shortage of mustard in France, which explains all the bare shelves in the supermarkets where the *moutarde* should be holding court. Some people have taken to hoarding the yellow condiment and some supermarkets have imposed a limit of one pot per person.

I had lived in Dijon for a year as a foreign language assistant and used to enjoy taking visitors around and extolling Dijon's fame as the mustard capital of the world. There is even a Maille shop in the centre of town with more than fifty different types of mustard. Imagine my *horreur* when Véronique told me that Dijon has not been the main supplier of mustard for years, and Canada accounts for as much as eighty per cent of the French supply. Worse: Maille is no longer an independent brand founded in 1747 with its coat of arms bearing the motto *Que Maille qui m'aille* (Maille is the only one for me) emblazoned on the lid. The brand is now owned by Unilever. The shortage of mustard is due to three factors: climate change, which has affected the production of the mustard seed in France and Canada; the war in the East has affected mustard exports from Ukraine and Russia; and the French passion for the condiment. Each French person consumes an average of one kilo of mustard every year. As one man lamented, 'France without mustard is like France without wine.' I beg to differ. The good news is that this year's mustard harvest has been abundant, so there are no shortages foreseen for next year. I have three different types of mustard in the fridge. *Au cas où* – just in case.

Vance, Véronique's husband who is an antiques dealer, came round a few days later to assess the damage to our old living room carpet and to advise if it could still be sent to auction. He noticed the *crédence*, the big wooden sideboard that has always been there in the house, against the living room wall, propped up on one side with books where the leg has disintegrated. Apparently, it comes from the "directoire" period between 1790 and 1810, just after the Revolution. Who knew there was anything of value in this house!

I had always been fascinated by the fact that the Revolution had torn up all the rules, even renaming the months and time. However, France had changed the calendar before, in 1564, under Charles IX, making 1 January the start of the year instead of 2 April. Soon, other countries followed suit. This is the reason why the tradition exists of making fun of people on 1 April as they were the ones who refused to recognise the new calendar.

***

Étienne Gouget, our wonderful neighbour, died at the end of May. Suzanne his widow, is frail and grief-stricken. When I ask about the dogs she answers, shaking her head, 'They died too.'

'And how about the chickens?' I ask, guessing the answer would be in a similar vein.

'The wild dogs from the village got them,' she replies, glumly.

Chickens have an unenviable fate. When I asked Mr Hermitman, another neighbour, how many chickens he had, he answered, 'Twenty. All destined for the *congélateur*, the freezer, in a week's time.

I always remember Étienne with his animals: cows, rabbits, sheep, chickens. In his later years, he divested himself of livestock and concentrated on the land. Apparently, Étienne's health was steadily deteriorating in the past year, and when it became clear to Étienne himself that he could no longer tend his beloved garden filled with vegetables, he took to his bed and faded away. Life indoors was not worth living.

I drive Suzanne over to St Eutrope cemetery to visit his grave. The family had refused to have a priest perform the burial ceremony. Suzanne explained bluntly, 'We are from the land; you live and die and that is it!' I suppose years of drowning cats, wringing the necks of ducks and chickens and killing sheep and rabbits have rendered a certain pragmatism necessary. The biggest plaque on Étienne's grave is from *La Société de Chasse*, the hunting association "La Diane", featuring an engraving of a hunter with a gun. All the local hunters paid homage to their fellow *chasseur*. Peasant farmers like Étienne viewed the hunt as a way to keep a check on Mother Nature. Hunting in France cannot be described as a rich man's pleasure activity.

Suzanne gives me a tour round the graveyard, pointing out the foibles and tales of all Étienne's new neighbours. 'We don't speak to them,' pointing at a nearby grave, 'and that's a young man who was only thirty when he fell off his tractor. His widow comes over regularly to visit him, but his mother comes nearly every day. And over there, that's my friend, Giselle; she died four months ago.' Suzanne's eyes fill with tears.

She wipes her face. *C'est pas gai, la vieillesse.* Old age is hard going. When I mentioned to her friend Odette, that I was worried about Suzanne, she answered prosaically: 'Every day is like a candle: some days it burns brightly, some days it merely flickers.'

We visit other friends whose parents have just died. I stock up on condolence cards and marvel at their formality and the enclosed adjoining card with a list of formulaic responses. The cards have come in very useful.

Temperatures have hit forty degrees and the land is burnt yellow, calling out for water. The farmers watch in despair as their crops fail and the leaves of the trees appear autumnal, brown and crinkled, until they too are burnt to a crisp. The fruit in our orchard has shrivelled up; none of my favourite fruit, *reine-claude*, greengages, have survived. The drought has escalated the *canicule*, the heatwave, and fires are burning in the nearby regions of Gironde and Les Landes. I panicked one day, when the smell of acrid smoke and a pall hung in the air and rushed over to check on Suzanne. She was surprised and dismissed my concern with a wave of her hand. 'Of course, I'm fine, these fires are far away; there is nothing to worry about. Since you are here, pull up a chair and watch *N'oubliez pas les paroles* with me.' Thus, I was ensconced for the evening, watching our favourite TV programme together. Suzanne gives me tomatoes from Étienne's vegetable garden, his beloved *potager*. They are bulbous and meaty, bursting with flavour. The box of eggs she gives me is a curious delight. The chickens belong to her daughter. Each of her chickens lays a different coloured egg. Every few evenings, I walk slowly down the track with Suzanne holding onto my arm. She is frightened to walk on her own, lest she fall over and there is no one to help her. I notice an enormous cauldron on the grass and ask her what it was used for. 'We boiled the pigs' carcasses in that.' She sighs. 'Those were the days.' I ask her if I could gather up some pinecones. I explain that they make perfect Christmas decorations. Suzanne looks at me curiously. 'Pinecones make the perfect firelighters,' she says. I dare not tell her that I buy firelighters from the supermarket. Me and my fancy, city ways.

My mother's friend Mimi had died earlier in the year. Mimi was irascible, sharp-tongued, contrary and kind. I had been very fond of her, and she had helped me so much going through all the hideous bureaucracy to secure Coutal. I felt guilty, because I hadn't seen her for the last two years, but Covid put paid to sociability.

Only last year, Étienne, Suzanne and our other neighbour Huguette, had lunch with me in Coutal. We lamented the fact that the ages were no longer published in the obituaries of the local paper. I was so busy the first few weeks of July, trying to fix all the things that didn't work, that I hadn't noticed the grim reaper flying overhead towards Huguette before I had a chance to say hello to her.

Suzanne was too ill to go to Huguette's funeral in St Eutrope, so Gerry and I did our best to find some passable sombre clothes to show our respects. We needn't have bothered. The church was packed out. Save one elderly man wearing a suit, tie and hat, everyone else was clad in jeans and T-shirts. We stuck out a mile, nay, a kilometre, as *les étrangers*. The sermon was completely without frills and anecdotes. Huguette was referred to as Huguette Birot, née Parrel, and the bare bones of her life story were read out: where she was born, lived, died and a sentence on her pastimes: cooking, breeding dogs, looking after her family. This was not the cheerful Huguette I remembered.

Although I had spoken to him on the phone, I had last seen Régis, Huguette's son, when he was seventeen, just as he had started his training as a gendarme. He had now been retired for the last seven years. Unexpectedly, he turned up at our house on the afternoon of his mother's funeral with his own adult son, because, as he explained, our presence at his mother's funeral had also been so unexpected and touching. We gave them a tour around the house. Régis had last been there about fifty years previously and remembered the cows – *les blondes d'Aquitaine* – in the byre. The very same byre that is now our living room. He was bowled over by the transformation!

Suzanne was still too ill to join the rest of the family for the placing of Huguette's ashes in the family tomb in St Vivien a few weeks later. I arrived alone and, again, stood out as the sole *étrangère*. The urn was placed next to her husband, Jean. Together they formed two pages of a book made out of granite. They had both died in their nineties, testimony to the healthy lifestyle they had led. I had an interesting conversation with the person from the funeral parlour. I asked why the ashes were not mixed together. After all, they had been such a loving couple. '*Ah non, c'est contre la loi!*' It is against the law! After all, who knows what went on in the secret life of married couples? And what about burying them in the garden? '*Ah non! C'est contre la loi!*' It is against the law! What if the house were sold? What about the remains in that case?

I persisted. What if it was the express wish for the person to be buried in the place they loved best? '*Ah non! C'est contre la loi!*' It's against the law! What if there was a dispute with the children (which often happened in French families), and one child refused to let the siblings visit the remains of the parents in the family garden? I had to admit he had a point there.

I changed tack. What if the person wished their ashes to be scattered over the mountains or buried at sea? At least the funeral man conceded that the law allowed sea funerals in certain cases, so many kilometres from the shore, but certainly people's ashes could not be chucked anywhere willy-nilly.

I had one last question. What if your express wish was that

some of your ashes were scattered in one place and some in another, that you were shared out, as it were.

'*Ah non, c'est contre la loi!*' It's against the law! You have to regard the ashes as sacred as they represent someone's body. You can't have an arm over there, a leg buried there...'

I wouldn't have minded, personally. He was losing patience with me, and I with him. This conversation was going down a conversational cul-de-sac. A sharp exit was required.

It is with trepidation that Gerry and I go to visit our old neighbour Blanche who entered the portals of the old folk's home just before the pandemic. This is her 102nd year and we are relieved to see her sweet smile and mischievous eyes. She is still the full shilling. She commiserates at the death of *jeune* – young – Étienne, whom she has known ever since he was a boy helping his father to paint her house. 'See that door over there?' She cocks her head to one side, indicating a door at the side of the old folk's reception area. 'That's where they put you if you lose your mind.' *Pour ceux qu'ils ont perdu la tête.* It was in the interest of the inmates to appear as compos mentis as possible. 'Nothing wrong with my brain,' said Blanche, tapping the side of her head. It would seem that compassion and empathy are not natural bedfellows.

'I am so glad you are alive, Sue!' Sue Castello is in her eighties, and it was not quite the welcome she expected from us. We visited her during a trip to *a vide grenier* (sparse pickings: one cocktail shaker and one wicker basket) near to her new home. It was not yet her home; she was still living in a caravan until her new home was built, and it was taking far longer than she had anticipated. She had not fared well in the searing heat and had spent a few days in hospital having her heart checked. '*C'est un coeur épuisé*,' said the doctor, tactlessly. It's a worn-out heart. 'It might be,' I countered, 'but at least it is still ticking. *Santé!*' We all drank to that.

In general, life expectancy in Aquitaine is higher than other parts of France; indeed, many go on till their nineties. Whenever I worry about the effects of age on my body, I remind myself of the artist Grayson Perry's dictum: "After fifty, a man should never pass a lavatory, never trust a fart and never waste an erection".

I expect there is a female equivalent.

***

Vide grenier season is here once again and Nicola and I return bargain hunting together. Nicola finds a cushion for me with an elephant motif and is still on the lookout for gargoyles for the barn wall. I brush down the walls in anticipation and a gargoyle falls on my forehead, leaving a large bruise. It lands on the very same spot that Gerry had dropped the car boot (accidently, I am reminded) two years previously. There is still no indentation; I must have leather skin. We chatted to one English stallholder who told us that he makes the rounds of all the *brocantes*, the *bric-a-brac* stalls, and he would be going to Monflanquin next Friday. Except he pronounced it as *Monn flann kwin*. Our eyebrows shot up with a quizzical, critical look.

The heat has a soporific effect on us all. We have been to few night markets. If you do not turn up early, then you miss out on the shade. I seek out swimming pools and siestas between cleaning one room at a time, ready for the constant stream of visitors. From time to time, I pop into Linda and Ian's swimming pool, on the pretext that I am the pool inspector, just there to check that it is always in tip-top condition. I give marks for cleanliness, the absence of beasties or leaves floating around, optimum temperature etc. Suffice to say they always get top marks. 'Fit for purpose,' I report back. Both inspector and those inspected are happy at the outcome. There has been a glut of courgettes, and Ian usually tries to foist some whoppers into my reluctant hands before I leave. I sternly warn him that he might be accused of bribery on the swimming pool front. I am not to be swayed, not by ubiquitous courgettes at any rate.

Ian converted his British driving licence to a French one when he was seventy-five and was told he had fifteen years worry-free driving. No one would check up on him until he was ninety! No wonder there are so many old, dangerous drivers around here!

For the first time in three years, I clean the windows, merrily humming George Formby's catchy ditty "When I'm Cleaning Windows". All I need is a ukulele. About the only time Gerry has left the final bedroom in the barn, is to pick up more building supplies. We occasionally catch up with friends. However, a deadline is a deadline. It's all in the prep.

Yet another year spent filling out a spreadsheet with the comings and goings of various people, where they are going to sleep and compiling the associated long shopping lists. At last, Rocco arrives with his human minders, David and Jane, at 3am. Brexit has made it very complicated and expensive to bring animals over to France. Rocco is usually a well-behaved and complacent dog, but the journey from Glasgow is a mind-numbingly long one.

Kathryn, our next visitor, has driven from Edinburgh, Mid Calder to be precise, all the way to Italy and stopped *chez nous* for a few days on the way home. Nevertheless, the following day, she is back in the car to visit the prehistoric cave paintings of Lascaux. I swear she has talons hooked to the gears of her car for smooth locomotion.

Eunice, Sharon's sister, heralds the arrival of all the other friends and family for Sharon's event. Eunice brings a matchbox with "Fuck the Government" printed on the top as a present. Rob, Sharon's husband, brings over boxes of British champagne, which is a bit like coals to Newcastle. 'Power through,' he advises us, cracking open the champagne mid-morning. No one wanders far from the house for the next three days. Thank God for siesta time. Everyone is having such a good time here that they do not even want to go to the *Bodega*, the big street party in Villeréal, the liveliest event in the year.

'I think all that went smoothly,' I say smugly to Gerry, just as things begin to go wrong. Rob's car makes a painful grinding noise on the road to Monflanquin, and we end up taking it to the nearest garage. A small stone had lodged itself between the brake pads. As it is such an easy operation to extract it, the mechanic merely asks for a note to be slipped into his hands, as a thank you, and then Rob happily tootles off north.

It had not even crossed my mind that there might be a problem buying a train ticket from Agen to Toulouse in advance for Naomi, Sharon's sister. However, I had not factored in the exodus of Parisians travelling south in August. I pleaded with the granite-faced harridan to let her at least stand in the carriage. '*Non!*' was the emphatic reply.

In fact, Eunice and I had planned to take Gerry out for lunch in Agen, as he has never been to the historic centre of the city before. For the last three years, Gerry has only visited the shopping centre on the outskirts for household and building supplies. It was not to be. I asked a taxi driver how much it would cost to take Naomi to Toulouse-Blagnac Airport, and he quoted €270. That could not be either. Therefore, we ended up driving Naomi to the airport, telling her not to call us if the 6pm flight to Edinburgh was delayed, which it was. She ended up arriving home in the early hours of the morning, only to find her beloved dog, Sasha, had just died. All credit to Naomi, she did not tell us straightaway. Meanwhile, Eunice,

Gerry and I carried out a smash-and-grab campaign at IKEA, bringing home curtains, blinds and an assortment of useless objects. Instead of a slap-up meal, Gerry tucked into dried-up meatballs the consistency of goats' gonads, before driving us back home.

Rocco was overjoyed to see us; we were less happy to see the state of his willy, with pus coming out of it. It was a desultory day.

We perked up the next morning. The internet was working; the sun was bright; Gerry applied ointment to Rocco's itchy bits; and we were reassured by Jill that Rocco had been bitten by the *aoûtats*, the pesky berrybug-like insects that come out in summer. I have had massive carbuncle on the tip of my nose, like Pinocchio, since the beginning of July. Except I have not been telling any lies. Is this a lie?

Nevertheless, we felt more chilled with only the three of us remaining: me, Gerry and Eunice. Our complacency was short-lived.

Our car was behaving in the same recalcitrant way as all its predecessors. 'Not another *voiture bien foutu*,' I wailed. Not another truly fucked car. I loved this Citroën car, with its leather seats. It was like driving a sofa. The garage sent out a vehicle recovery truck and our car was duly dispatched to their forecourt. Initially, we were hopeful. It was all about finding another 2003 model automatic gearbox. Luckily, Jill and Simon lent us their Mini Cooper until we had our car fixed. Time was running out as the garage was about to close for a fortnight for their annual summer holidays. Gerry and I trawled the countryside, France, the world, for the elusive gearbox. The response was always the same, the equivalent of "give up hope all ye who enter here". How many cars have we sent to the great rust heap in the sky? I'm losing count.

To bolster our spirits, Eunice upped the bar by concocting

the most succulent margaritas to celebrate being alive in this sunny place. Jill and Simon came over to partake of the libation. They needed to borrow the Mini Cooper back for the morning to transport the slaughtered pig they had bought, and Jill was excitedly discussing how many sausages it would provide. Then disaster again. Mr Pigman phoned up in great distress to say that there had been a break-in at the piggery and all the pigs had been stolen! This called for another round of margaritas as well as a round of *bons mots*. "Better send the pigs on them". "Best not make any rash decisions". "Utter swine". "Bet they make a pig's ear of it". "Who's telling porky pies?".

Not long after, we noticed an advert for a motorised pig roaster for sale nearby, a mere €400. It can be added to the communal longing to join with the giant elephant hanging in the barn and the vintage fire engine, previously listed for sale by a neighbour. All the things we hanker after but cannot have.

Eunice fared slightly better on her return home. After she had been herded with all the other passengers into the holding pen, the announcement was made that the plane was delayed for a few hours. There were only a few seats available in the departure lounge, so Eunice stretched out on the floor and closed her eyes, waiting for deliverance, or at least to ascend into the sky.

Gerry returns to Glasgow for work. Someone has to do it, I remind him. It's now me and Rocco, home alone. Suzanne remarks that Rocco is getting fat and I explain that it has been difficult to walk an old dog with a thick coat in this heat. But I take her words to heart, and as soon as rain falls, we are out, seeking puddles where Rocco can plonk his undercarriage and muddy his paws. His paws make a click-click sound when he walks because his claws are now too long. He requires the attrition of the asphalt, and not all this soft padding around the countryside. Most mornings we go on our usual walk: past our wood, past craggy island house, past the house with the demented blind dog and down the village path. Rocco is usually in full olfactory mode, nose to the ground. So much so, that he often does not notice the deer gambolling in the nearby fields. Occasionally, when he is whiffy, I take him swimming in a local lake. Sadly, Rocco has been banned from swimming pools as he leaves a trail of black fur on the surface of the water. In his old age, Rocco has fallen in love with Jiji, also a black Labrador of the same vintage. Her owner, Anne, calls Jiji a tart, as she knocks Rocco to the ground and dances around him, for hours, in a balletic trance, the doggy equivalent of the dance of the seven veils. Puppy love. I have never seen Rocco so happy, a spring in his paws.

I dream that in my old age I acquire a Bichon Frisé, a French lapdog, white, frilly, poodely, usually with silk ribbons around its neck, very popular with old ladies in cities. However, my dream is that they make perfect hot water bottles for the winter. I wake up to find myself cuddling my pillow. I am surprised that this was actually the case for the French royal family some centuries back, who would pop into bed warmed up by these frou-frou dogs.

Charlotte lives nearby and also lets us partake of her pool. As a present, she gives us two stained-glass panels for the barn bedrooms. We are still looking for one last pane to replace the Perspex and newspaper temporary solution in one outside window. Before this can be done, a big storm, more like a tornado, hurls in overnight. Ron says he has never encountered a storm with such force in the forty years he has had a house here. I wake up in shock as hailstones whip through the gaps of the Perspex and land on my face, then clods of earth spatter my face, then a trembling Rocco jumps on top of me into the bed. It takes a few minutes to come to.

There is an enormous noise outside and I think that a tree has fallen onto the barn roof. In-between flashes of lightning, I witness garden furniture hurtling down the track, branches falling down, but luckily no damage to our home. Others are not so lucky; forty plum trees have been ripped out at the back of the house, the plum harvest ruined, cables down and roofs collapsed. I lie in bed, clutching the dog until the violence of the elements die down. *Why didn't the storm strike all the hideous leylandii at the foot of the road, oppressive light thieves? Smite them with all its force*, I think crossly. Miraculously, the wooden well cover has still not collapsed inwards. Carefully, I remove plank after plank and the sound of a big splash is averted. The well had been rebuilt ten years previously by the amorously named builder Mr Lustalot. I'm sure his name alone brought him in extra work, if only by sheer curiosity.

The storm reminded me of the one we experienced two years before when Gerry and I travelled down from Glasgow. We were beset by a similar belter just an hour away from Coutal. Gerry had reminded me that there was "no need to panic". The car is essentially a "Faraday cage", a metal box which protects passengers from electric charges, such as lightning. This didn't stop him from insisting that I had to get out of the car to remove all the detritus on the road. I was the moving target.

The impact of the hikes in the price of energy is far lower in France than in Britain, despite the civil unrest it has engendered. The largely state-owned electricity supplier, EDF, has offered discounts, and the government has capped any rise to four per cent. At the end of June, we ordered a state-of-the-art wood-burning stove for the barn (I reckoned if it was good enough for a Norwegian winter, it was good enough for us) and discovered that it would be delivered in six months' time, as demand has tripled since the price rise. 'Before Christmas?'

'Hopefully yes,' Mr Stoveman answered.

I feel relieved that our Glasgow flat is tiny, and our energy costs are commensurate with its size. Nevertheless, we can manage our energy consumption far more easily in France. If need be, in the winter, we can move into the old part of the house where the living room is heated by a log-burning stove and the old kitchen has a very old, but fully functioning, wood-burning cooking stove. I have ordered a truckful of oak logs which will arrive in the next two weeks. I'm now looking at the branches felled by the recent storm with heightened interest.

You win some, you lose some. House insurance is only valid in France if you have a certificate proving that you have had all your chimneys swept: this is an annual occurrence costing €75 per chimney. For years, my mother refused to believe that this was the case, and as a consequence, our house has been uninsured for most of the time our family has lived here. She believed that since Mr FireExtinguisher man comes every summer to check the extinguishers, that the fire check is covered. Our chimneysweeps come in three generations: the grandfather, the father and the son. It is a spectacle to witness as father chimney sweep walks down the spine of the roof, balancing the pole in his hands, with assurance and agility, rather like Charles Blondin crossing the Niagara Falls in 1859.

At the end of August, the tourists start to melt away, as do the street parties and festivals. There is the odd blip, when the star act of the Monflanquin medieval festival, the live American Eagle, simply disappears during the bird show. No amount of meat could tempt him back. A medieval festival in the blistering heat of August? All that chainmail and armour clanking around, delightfully bonkers.

Irena, my daughter, arranges a house party here for eight of her friends from London. She arrives a week early, to prepare the house, buy in the food and drink and generally titivate the place to her satisfaction, at the same time as working "remotely". I call her "my wee scrubber". She constantly rearranges objects for their maximum aesthetic impact. Joyfully, she picks up treasures from the *vide greniers* and *brocantes*. I no longer know where anything is in the house. 'Where is the rosemary, Mum?'

'There it is, interspersed in the hedge of lavender, swamped by the brambles,' I answer. I dare her to ask why I have not cut down the brambles. It is on the long list of the things for which I will kill people, if mentioned. Wisely, Irena says nothing, interpreting the glowering look on my face correctly. She is stressed out by the weather forecast, which predicts rain and thunder. I explain that the forecast changes constantly, usefully veering to bright and sunny at the last minute. This is not Scotland, after all. In the event, the weather is *scorchio* and Coutal party central is a success.

I have been *papped oot*, ejected, from my home for the four-day duration of the party. I hasten to say, that it is of my own volition. Linda and Ian treat me to a holiday at their house where I sleep, eat, rest, swim, read and chat. I am thoroughly cossetted. I have every excuse to do as little as possible, because I have no car for a week. No car, no home, no dog, no job. Bliss. My responsibilities are rapidly disappearing. My only obligation is to walk Rocco for an hour in the morning and leave him back in the house to join the snoozing occupants. The whole operation takes just under three hours, and I fling myself into the pool on my return. Rocco cannot accompany me to Ian and Linda's because of the resident cats. I suspect he is knackered by the round-the-clock merriment back home. Indeed, I am told that he is joining in with every game of table tennis, barking and running from each end of the table to the other. When I eventually return home, the guests have all returned to London and normal life resumes. Rocco sleeps for two whole days, rousing himself only to eat and attend to his bodily functions.

My own stress was the violation of our very sensitive septic tank. We had a scare when a previous visitor had used bleach to clean the toilets and we feared the whole fragile micro-system was imploding. I bored Irena continuously, reminding her no wet wipes, no sanitary towels, not *anything* but human waste and toilet paper were to go down the toilet. The microbes were quite happy with doses of yoghurt. The lesson had obviously got through because plastered all over the bathrooms were big signs saying "POO, PISS, PAPER ONLY PLEASE". I wonder which parent the girl gets her tact and diplomacy from?

I had imagined my new life full of art classes and pottery workshops, but it has not worked out that way. Apart from the weekly Pilates class, leisure is limited. I try to write, "'my expensive hobby", as my cousin Zeina terms it. I yearn to write my favourite words in one sentence, "thrice, whence and thence" in context. At least, I lecture myself, write to cover the costs of writing. I may not always be a member of the *salon des refuseés*. The scrapping of the Net Book Agreement, whereby writers were paid a minimum amount, means that it is nearly impossible to make a living from writing. Writing, I sternly remind myself, makes sense of my life. I should regard it as a pleasure. It does not always have to be a rich person's pastime; we cannot all self-publish like Robert Graves and Virginia Woolf, who effectively set up their own printing presses. Writing, for me, at this stage in my life, creates order and routine. I should leave it at that.

***

I need a project in which to thoroughly immerse myself. When I was asked if I would help with setting up a film festival in one of the *bastides*, it was the divertissement I was looking for. No pay? Wayhay. Bickering in the ranks? You are talking my language. Art for art's sake.

It was a great idea to help boost the local economy after Covid; after all, Castillonnès has one of the oldest cinemas in France, as well as other venues for events. It has the accolade: *les plus beaux villages de France*. One of the most beautiful villages in France, alongside many of its neighbours.

If Cannes, can do it, so can we. There was the small matter of little money, and so fundraisers were required. Together with Linda, we produced the Castifilmquiz in English and French. Ian and Eunice manned the bar. I had brought over a Tunnock's bonanza as prizes, but when Linda and I unpacked it, we discovered that the mice had beaten us to the chocolate delights. As they had done with the argan soap before, the mice had carefully (and artfully) munched just a corner of each prize. We gathered all the untouched prizes and locked them in a tin box until the fundraiser. I encountered a mouse with a brass neck. I noticed a piece of bread at the corner of the kitchen worktop and tried to pick it up, but a mouse got there before me, on the other side of the worktop where he could not be seen, and tried to snatch it from me. I was in a tussle with a mouse! Simon says that when you see one mouse, you know there is a family of twenty behind it. Linda fished out a carton of mouse killer to discover that half the cardboard was already munched at the bottom. This called for Mice Wars, rather like *Loir* Wars, when Sharon and Eunice unleashed an all-out attack on dormice a few years back. We bought the most toxic solution we could find, that had the word *radicale* on the carton, and soon, all evidence of mice was eradicated.

Just as Yvonne and Fran arrive at Bergerac, and the film festival is launched, Queen Elizabeth dies and Britain is plunged into darkness and a sea of cellophaned flowers.

Seventeen

When I Jump

It's impossible,
said pride.
It's risky,
said experience.
It's pointless,
said reason.
Give it a try,
whispered the heart.

Anon

I am nearly thirteen years old. I am sitting awkwardly on the wooden slats of the roof. I look pensive, quizzically squinting in the sunlight. I don't think the lack of health and safety equipment bothers me at all. I have plastic gloves on which suffice for the task to hand: removing the old, broken Roman tiles and replacing them with the latest version. I am still a girl, on the cusp of glowering, truculent teenage years. At this moment, my complexion is clear, and my hair has turned dark blonde. I am content in my own cocoon. I am not yet fully formed, and the plasticity of my brain is busy amassing information. Nevertheless, I am uninformed in so many ways. At this moment, my life is full of possibilities, my future yet to unfold like the unfolding landscape in front of me. The open rolling countryside, devoid of new buildings which will soon spring up, the trees, pinpricks below, before they grow and swallow this glorious vista. I am careful not to slip and fall, which would entail an accident. But if I were to jump, it would be an act of my own volition, a clear statement of intent. For this reason, I avoid walking near the edge of cliffs; there is something ridiculously tempting. For one fleeting second, to submit to this feeling of total abandonment. I will not jump, I rebuke myself. There is a life here to live and promises to fulfil. My father is taking this photograph. He is precariously standing on one of the top rungs of the ladder he has made himself. He holds the camera firmly with both hands. He is concentrating hard. 'Look at me,' he says. He is far more at risk of falling than I am.

I am well used to climbing, the higher the tree the better, from one bough to the next. Young limbs extending, clinging, swinging, grasping and hauling myself right to the top. It would never occur to me that I could fall, that potential danger lies in this activity. I blithely ignore the "Keep Out Danger" signs which surround the crumbling walls of the château on the hill above Coutal Haut. Madame Birot, who had sold Coutal Haut to us, had her wedding in this once grand venue, I recall her telling me once. There is no ceiling now and very little left of the wooden floor where people danced and glasses clinked in a toast, *Santé*! I scamper around the carcass of what remains of this place, hoping fruitlessly to discover some treasure, but it had all been picked clean many years before. I have gone upmarket in my foraging.

Relics of accidents cover my skin like talismans. My body has protected me from unseen disaster, leaving burns and scars on the surface, reminders of whatever happened. They have gone and are now healed. Before I was five years old, I was exceptionally accident-prone. (After the age of five, I simply was accident-prone, in a monotonous fashion.) Once, after a bath and drying myself with a towel in front of the fire, my mother took my hands and swung me round and round. I laughed gleefully, then suddenly my hands slipped out of her grasp and I hurtled into the fire, landing on the hot coals. My laughter quickly turned into screams of agony, and I put my hands on the coals to push myself off this pyre. My mother, horrified, swaddled me in the towel and slathered my burnt skin with soothing lotion and bandages. I was mummified. For weeks to come, whenever I needed to go to the toilet, I had to summon a handmaiden from my family to carefully unwrap the bandages from the barbecue of seared flesh, lower me on my throne, my bandaged hands outstretched. When I had finished my business, like some old hag, I would yell, '*Weczy pupa!*' – Wipe my bottom! Then the process of remummification would resume.

Apart from the usual scrapes and falls that resulted in an accumulation of scabs on knees and elbows, there was one event that could be termed as a near out-of-body experience. I was so intent on the important task of catching bumblebees in a glass jar, that I hadn't noticed an obstacle in my path. I tripped, fell and the jar smashed on the ground. The glass exploded into a kaleidoscope of sharp shards as the angry bees zigzagged up into the air. I felt distinctly like an observer; I felt the slice of the glass as it severed the veins in my left wrist and coolly watched, detached, as the blood gushed out like water from a burst pipe. Who would have known this body could contain so much liquid? My father had just returned from a business trip to America. My mother roused him from his jet-lagged state. He pulled his trousers over his pyjamas and drove us manically to the hospital. I sat in the back seat, my head leaning back, exhausted with this never-ending pantomime, somehow anaesthetised from the pain as my mother wrapped layer upon layer of bandage around my wrist which would soak up bright red in a matter of seconds. Years later, I attended a job interview. I thought it was going surprisingly well; the requisite responses came readily to my lips, bouncing back to the interviewer's questions, as he nodded, encouragingly. Then something happened; he frowned, and the hitherto pleasant exchange lost its upbeat tone. I was momentarily nonplussed and then I saw his eyes had fixed on my wrist when I had gesticulated to make a point. The light shining through the window had highlighted the silver scar, filigree, a sliver of moon, and I knew that this man had concocted a backstory in his head that didn't exist. 'No, no,' I wanted to tell him. 'You've got this completely wrong. I'm not some sort of person who tried to top herself. I'm a thoroughly rational, competent person, fit for purpose. I can explain this; don't back off – I want the job!' The interview ended soon after; I was informed that there were many candidates, and I would receive notification soon if I had been successful. *Fat chance*, I thought as I walked out, feeding a lifelong aversion to interviews.

***

Children of my era were always out playing in the street, ball games (*the old grey mare she ain't what she used to be, ain't what she used be, ain't what she used to be... ever since the old man died…*) skipping, Chinese ropes (*jingle jangle silver bangle, jingle jangle out*), "beds", with a "peever", usually a flat stone. I learnt later that others called this game hopscotch. I would be forever playing on wasteland, twisted vestiges of an industrial past, making dens in the undergrowth. Later, in our house in Lot-et-Garonne, we would play in a nearby deserted village all day and come home when the light faded and we were hungry.

The game I loved the best was racing in "bogeys". These were clumsily assembled carts from bits of wood and metal nailed together (reluctant adults had to be summoned to help in the construction), and we would whizz down the steepest road in our latter-day chariots, oblivious to any traffic that had the temerity to stray into our path. I graduated from this to my yellow tricycle and then to the state-of-the-art Raleigh bike, cycling down the same steep road as fast as I could. One day, the inevitable happened and a car passed in my line of vision. It was close enough to see the look of shock on the driver's face as he slammed on his brakes, as I almost slid under the tyres. After checking that I wasn't injured, he hurled pent-up abuse at this stupid child who could have got herself killed. I limped home, pushing my bike with the usual suspects of scabby knees and skinned limbs. I graduated, as an adult, to a couple of car crashes where, miraculously, I emerged with bruises and scratches from a jungle of metal and shattered glass to smooth myself down.

My mother despaired at my clumsiness, my seeming lack of awareness of danger. After Polish school on a Saturday, she would often take us to her friend's restaurant, Epicures, for a treat. One day, I ran in through the open door. Except it wasn't open – the glass had just been cleaned – and, like a cartoon character, I reeled back after the full force of the impact left me stunned and bleeding. The gash on my forehead healed into a translucent moon sliver that has paled in the ensuing years.

***

I first visited Lebanon at the end of the long seventeen-year-old civil war. The country was still in shock, a ravaged battlefield. Numerous glimpses of the Phoenician past, a mosaic, a colonnade, popped out unexpectedly from torn tarmac. At last, I visited Baalbek, the ancient site of temples and stones. Baalbek makes the Acropolis look like a pile of pebbles There were only a handful of tourists wandering around. A friend of my cousin, Saadin, offered to take me on a tour of the country and proudly wheeled out the barely used car from the garage. It didn't take long to discover that the brakes were faulty, as we hurtled headlong down pockmarked steep passes overlooking the Mediterranean. I gripped the edge of my seat tightly, muttering some half-forgotten prayer, amazed at Saadin's insouciance, his cigarette casually dangling as he chatted about the topography and history of the land of milk and honey. When he noticed my anxiety, he laughed and said, 'It's OK, the car will slow down naturally, inshallah, due to the disrepair and potholes in the road. There is no need to worry at all. Ah, here is Walid Jumblatt's stronghold; let us partake in a glass of cardamom coffee. That will calm your nerves.'

Despite my earlier experiences, I was not afraid of travelling all over Scandinavia for a month on a Eurorail pass, continually meeting up with the same glum-faced Japanese tourists, in some cold waiting room, in Narvik or Finnmark early in the morning, waiting for a train connection. I was not afraid of hitchhiking alone through Europe. Although I ask myself what madness was going through my head, I was more bemused than afraid at finding myself standing beside a leopard in Africa (we just looked at each other up and down) until the animal moved off.

***

Back on the canal, my kayak tips over unexpectedly. It doesn't seem like it at the time, but with hindsight, it was third time lucky. I'm not too far from the house; maybe Gerry will see me from the window. For a second, I do nothing; maybe it will right itself. We bought the kayak second-hand for £50; it is an old model, a vintage kayak, made from fibreglass, sleek, long, narrow and bright red. I *shoogle* around; the kayak roll is easy, I have been told, yet nothing is happening. I am wearing my favourite blue woollen jumper, and the weight of the saturated material is pulling me down. I realise now that I have foolishly clambered into the kayak the wrong way round and my legs are trapped in the narrow funnel, and no matter how hard I try to move them, they wedge themselves further in. I have not taken the massive gulp of oxygen I need from the outset to get me out of this predicament. My lungs are bursting, no air in the bellows; I am lightheaded and starting to panic. I don't want to drown in this canal outside my house. I write this and think of Sharon's words. 'Darlink, I'm being waterboarded again.' Then, with some almighty superhuman effort, I manage to dislodge my legs and ferverishly push and surface, spluttering, eyes bulging, with rasping sounds emerging from my throat. I would not have drowned. A couple walking on the canal path have noticed the turn of events and are anxiously waiting for me to pop out beside the upturned kayak, and when I do not, they are ready to jump in and rescue me. They haul me out and check I am unharmed. Apart from my bleeding and bruised legs and general state of shock, I am indeed unharmed. Again, I have outwitted my own foolishness, and life has gathered me up in its arms again, as one of its own, albeit errant, chicks. Cluck cluck, tsk, tsk, I should know better. All this is my own doing and negligence; there is no one to blame but myself.

I am not brave, but I can be reckless. Impulsive. I have no concept of a bad outcome and yet there have been times that I have been truly afraid, a true *feartie*. I am afraid of being in Coutal alone, with its creaking and its moans whispering through the night, its many ghosts sweeping around the walls and percolating my febrile mind, playing tricks on me.

I dream that Sharon and I are driving in a convertible, hood down, hair flying in the wind, laughing jubilantly. 'Let's get nearer the edge of the cliff,' she says. The full vertiginous drop. 'It is our *Thelma and Louise* swan song. Let's go crashing down; let the ocean embrace us, smithereens on the rocks.' The longed-for defenestration. That tiny voice that tells you to jerk the steering just a tiny bit and take a flying leap, *l'appel du vide*.

The grim reaper will have to wait for some other year. He will have to get on with his autumnal duties in Aquitaine, chopping the crone-like stalks and seedheads of the sunflowers. Blackened and stooped, their shining bright time has passed.

I am not ready. The sublime Icarus moment slips by.

When I jump, oh I hope many years from now, I will embrace the lightness of being; I will be a fully formed, protean and informed thing, following the curvature of the Earth.

The party is not over yet. *Que la fête commence.*

Eighteen

Gaudeamus Igitur *Therefore, Let Us Rejoice*

We are going to die, and that makes us the lucky ones. Most people are never going to die because they are never going to be born. The potential people who could have been here in my place, but who will in fact never see the light of day, outnumber the sand grains of Arabia. Certainly, those unborn ghosts include greater poets than Keats, scientists greater than Newton... In the teeth of these stupefying odds, it is you and I, in our ordinariness, that are here. We privileged few, who won the lottery of birth against all odds, how dare we whine at our inevitable return to that prior state from which the vast majority have never stirred?

Richard Dawkins

It would be wonderful to live to a good old age, mobility and marbles more or less intact, tottering to the very end, glass in hand.

Memories are captured like flies in amber, holding fast. If only we could live in the moment and distil each last drop of pleasure.

From the top of my head, tonight:

Swimming on my back outside, feeling the warmth of the post meridian sun

Banquet – the first time we stayed in Hipping Hall in the Lake District

The whooshing sound of vacuum cleaners and washing machines

Small children sleeping in the parental bed

The salty smell of Rocco after he has been swimming in the sea

Goutal aftershave

The paintings of Marc Chagall, the whites of Sorolla

Whenever the mood takes me: David Bowie, Lou Reed, Chopin's nocturnes and preludes, Natacha Atlas, Stabat Mater, Fairuz, David Balfe: I have a love and it will never fade away, Karine Polwart's "The Lost Words Blessing", Bob Dylan: "Oh, Sister", Jackie Kay's poem, *Fiere*, about friendship

Gin & bitter lemon

Mediterranean culinary delights – 'Bring on Sicilian lemons,' says Sharon

'Remember,' said Auntie Margaret, 'that the Japanese believe that Inari the fox god, fornicates under our fingernails'

Spotting Mount Fuji looming in sight like a giant ice cream

Red Samian ware from Vindolanda, the ingeniousness of the Romans

My elder sister and I in Beatles pudding bowl haircuts

dancing in front of the black-and-white TV in the living room: *I love you, yeah yeah yeah*

A Lady Taking Tea, Jean Chardin. Hunterian Art Gallery, Glasgow. Complete contemplation

Stretching out on a mossy bank, the tinkling sound of a burn below, dappled sunshine filtered through the trees

Elephants and swans

The coconut smell of gorse

My *Babcia* (my father's mother) saying that you always have to have the sun in your heart

My *Dziadzia* (my mother's father) – his name on the walls of Kelvingrove Art Gallery & Museum – one name out of many benefactors

My *Moosh* (mother) – her delicious cooking. Why did she never open a restaurant?

Rocco playing with other dogs, the sheer abandonment to pleasure, of being in the moment. Dogs know all about mindfulness

Working in Alexandra township – the postman singing to his young daughter strapped on his back – a pupil singing the aria to *Madama Butterfly* on the steps of the high school to welcome us

Wrapped up with a good book that makes you want to stay on the sofa all day

Gerry and I watching telly of an evening, a glass of wine to hand

Walking around Stromboli, smelling the sulphur of the volcano

Crunching through snow on Mount Etna

Looking at Munch's *The Scream* but only seeing a poorly drawn spaniel instead

Irena and Ziggy, when they were wee, giggling as

they chuck tiny pebbles through the restaurant
courtyard window of Hôtel de l'Europe in
Villeréal, the plopping sound as the pebbles land
in the customers' soup – time for a sharp exit
Salted caramel ice cream
The ritual of the stereo, the stylus jumping so that
memories of favourite tracks are slightly marred
– wish you were here – *jump* – we're just – *jump* –
lost souls swimming in a fish – *jump* –, year after
year

***

Time for vespers
I am travelling in my mind. A terrific distance.

EPILOGUE

The Romans did not have a word for grey; it was either dark green or dark blue. How exotic. They obviously had not stuck around long enough in Glasgow on a wet December day.

Curiosity gets the better of us and we turn up at Susan and Mike's ground-floor flat in Clouston Street in Glasgow's West End and ask the significance of these two-kilometre stones outside their flat. Mike explains that he lived in France for a number of years and on a trip to see a friend in Sigoulès, he spotted the stones in a big heap with many others, ready to be tossed into landfill sites. 'If they had just sold them at auction, can you imagine how much it would earn for the commune?' asks Mike. He managed to lift two of the stones into his van with his friend, but when they returned for the rest, they had already disappeared.

Nevertheless, here are the stones, intact, a little part of Aquitaine, in Glasgow's West End.

A constant reminder of home.

SCOTTISH GLOSSARY

bahookie	n. backside
batter	v. to beat up
bluitered	adj. drunk, having been hit or kicked hard
breeks	n. trousers
cheeky bizom	n. light-hearted riposte: cheeky so-and-so
close	n. tenement building
cludgie	n. toilet
hee-haw	adv. nothing
hoo-ha	n. commotion
hooley (blawn a hooley)	n. wild and windy weather
feartie	n. coward
foosty a	dj. in a decayed state or smell
gie (givin') it laldy	v. to sing or do proudly, with great gusto

guddle	n. mess, muddle, confusion. Toilsome dirty, messy work
jag	n. jab (of needle)
nary a body	pro. no one
peely-wally	adj. sickly, feeble, pallid, delicate
scorchio	adj. hot weather
scunnered	adj. annoyed, discontented, bored, fed up
sook	v. to suck, n. teacher's pet
squee-wiff	adj. off kilter, off centre
stoor	n. dust
stooshie	n. an uproar, hubbub, disturbance
tablet	n. Scottish version of fudge
wee	adj. small

FRENCH GLOSSARY

---

attestation (f) official paper required during Covid lockdown to prove you were on official business

au secours! help!

claie (f) old-fashioned plum dryer

commune (f) local parish

co-voiturage (m) car-sharing

les guerres des chariots (fpl) trolley wars (in supermarkets)

déchetterie (f) rubbish dump

distributeur (m) baguette machine

hors de combat out of action

fouine (f) stone marten

garde à l'eau watch out (water being chucked out)

hors de service not working

loir (m) dormouse

mairie	(f) town hall
miam miam	yum yum
ouaf ouaf	woof woof
punaise	(f) type of local bug
à la recherche du	
vide perdu	pun on Proust's *à la recherche du temps perdu* (remembrance of times past)
il y a des gifles qui	
manquent!	someone deserves a slap but does not receive one
Si l'on me presse de dire pourquoi je l'aimais, je sens que cela ne se peut exprimer qu'en répondant: 'Parce que c'était elle, parce que c'était moi.	
Pun on Montaigne's	famous reflection on the power of friendship after the death of his best friend, Étienne de La Boétie,(*parce que c'était lui, parce que c'était moi*)
Plus ça change, plus	
ç'est la même chose	the more things change, the more they stay the same

PERMISSIONS

Advice sought from copyright sources for permission to quote, where appropriate. I acknowledge and thank them for inspiring me.

Guidelines from The Copyright and Rights in Performances (Quotation and Parody) Regulations 2014 www.legislation. gov.uk.

REFERENCES AND QUOTATIONS

Big Bird, *Sesame Street*, quotation
Guillaume Apollinaire, Refrain from "Le Pont Mirabeau", *Alcools* Collection
Robert Burns, "Ae Fond Kiss"
Rod Argent, "She's Not There"
Tom Leonard, poem
Alexandra Hall Hall, Twitter thread
Glasgow motto on Glasgow's coat of arms
Edwin Muir, "Strawberries"
John Roderick Bannerman, "Mairi's Wedding", Scottish folk song
John Denver, "You fill up my senses. (Annie's Song)"
Sydney Carter, "Lord of the Dance"
Lennon-McCartney, "Lucy in the sky with diamonds"
Rodgers & Hammerstein, "Some enchanted evening"

Arlen &Harberg, "Over the Rainbow"
Robert Calvert & Dave Brock, "Silver Machine"
Archbishop Desmond Tutu, quotation
Irvine Welsh, quotation, *The National* 16 May 2021
John Bunyan, "The Pilgrim"
Joseph Beuys, commentary on "Aktions"
Sean Scully, review of Giorgio Morandi's *Resistance and Persistence*
Alasdair Gray, epithets on stone, Forth and Clyde Canal
John Kerry, quotation
Roger Waters, "Wish you were here"

ACKNOWLEDGEMENTS

Many thanks to my tip-top *tía*, Yvonne Blair, who rightly curtailed some flights of fancy and whose help was invaluable. Soon it will be fannying-around time.

Thanks to Sue Malthouse and Vicky McGraw for giving so generously of their time to help shape this flabby beast.

Thanks to Alison Hill, good at saying yes to all my requests.

Thanks as ever to the Schemies and "Swan Watchers", Fran Cunningham and Jen Smith. And, of course, as always, Gerry Coutts.

Thanks to Ann Fairfull, Susan Belkacemi, Sarah Kouzi, Bill Quick, Sonia Baird, Rosemary Carr, Elaine Rennie-Mclean, Liana Marletta, Christine Bovill, Lena Simons, Zeina Kouzi, Cristina Hernández, Nicola Almond, Bridget & Keith Turner, Norma Eedle, Iain Anderson, Ian Herbert, Linda Hamer,

Jill Foxley and Jennie Whetton, for all their practical help, support and encouragement.

Thanks to the team at Troubador for their help and professionalism.

I think I'm getting the hang of this now.
Du pain, du fromage, du vin, duvet.

Facebook page: https://www.facebook.com/BasiaGordonWriter
Email: basiag17@hotmail.com

 Matador

For exclusive discounts on Matador titles,
sign up to our occasional newsletter at
troubador.co.uk/bookshop